Reflections
from
Miri's Woods

by
Ron Scott

Softcover
ISBN 9781-5213460-4-4

Reflections
from
Miri's Woods

Contents

Reaching Out

Odd Ends

A Last Look

Preface

For more than ten years I served as editor of the newsletter of the St. Louis Psychological Association. My tenure resulted largely from a lack of competition: I served a year as President, and assumed responsibility for the newsletter, because no one else wanted to do those jobs.

Such volunteer roles usually offer few rewards. The role did, however, provide me with a singularly important benefit: a platform. So for some thirty years, beginning as I approached 50, I have been able to comment, relatively unencumbered, on events in my life and the lives of those around me. Those reflections have touched on issues relating to members of my family, my profession, and my community, although in one way or another they all ultimately had to do with me. For this reason I have come to understand them as "memoiristic," in the broadest sense of that term. Perhaps an "episodic memoir," composed of "brief personal essays," is not too pretentious a label for what follows.

Far too many persons helped, in one way or another, in the creation of these reflections and this book to be credited or, for that matter, even remembered. Certainly, appreciation must be extended to the leaders of the St. Louis Psychological Association who allowed me to retain space in the newsletter and, with it, my self-appointed platform. In addition, comments by Association members about specific columns, or about how much they enjoyed my writing, was a continuing source of motivation. Gratitude is also extended to Rockwell Gray and the students in his Washington University writing classes who seemed to appreciate me and my writings. It was within the framework of Rockwell's "Memoir Writing" class that I discovered what it was that I had been trying to do all those years; and the project assignment of that class provided the structure needed to begin to put this book together.

And I must, of course, express gratitude to the various characters – friends, family members and others – given starring and cameo roles in these pages. One cannot *have* a story, much less tell it, without such persons. I am certainly conscious that in most cases they have not known that they were being appropriated for my purposes. I can only hope that they will not be displeased with the results.

Several people have been specifically instrumental in helping the production of this book, and deserve much more than mere mention. Ginger Cockerham, a personal coach who helped me define purpose and maintain focus, was particularly helpful. More recent support has come from Barbara Levin's gentle nudges, and from Will Ridley.

Finally, more gratitude than I can ever express is reserved for my wife, Marilyn, who, in addition to reading most portions of this book as they were being written over the years, and listening to endless obsessions about what I was trying to do, has given the most valuable gift a writer can receive: actually appreciating what I've tried to say. In a very real sense this book is dedicated to her.

All of the selections in this collection originally appeared as columns in the newsletter between 1988 and 2004, in the month noted below each selection title. The introductory essays to each section are new; and a few columns have been reprinted in other professional newsletters, but none have been otherwise published. A second collection of later columns and other writings is being compiled foir publication in the near future.

Ron Scott
May, 2017

A Look Ahead

Miri's Woods

It's a matter of perspective, really. Deep thoughts do not necessarily require deep woods.

Almost thirty years ago, after the kids had (we thought) gone out on their own, we moved into a smaller home along a little tree-lined stream in west St. Louis County. The entire wooded strip, including meandering stream and trees on either bank, was less than a hundred feet across; but in the summertime, when we first saw the property, it was thick with trees and leaves and provided a tableau as if of deep woods.

We were entranced, even though many of the trees were removed by the electric company, which owned the land the stream flowed through, to run power lines. It was a delightfully idyllic spot in the midst of an area spotted with subdivisions, condos and strip malls. Over the years, sitting on our little deck, we saw and heard deer, wild turkey, and other animals and birds too numerous to identify.

It also was a good place to think. Deep thoughts, after all, do not necessarily require deep woods.

I had just turned fifty when we moved to Miri's Woods (an unofficial name coined in honor of our first grandchild). By the age of fifty, if one is paying any sort of attention at all, life should be starting to make at least a little sense.

It isn't that I haven't had opportunities to figure things out; it's just that I've always felt so . . . *naive*. Having grown up on a farm, lived on both coasts (as well as in the Midwest), garnered degrees in religion, history and psychology, and worked as a banker, welfare worker, parole agent, work-release center supervisor, college teacher, and psychotherapist (while acquiring two wives, five children and six grandkids), Lord knows I ought to have learned something.

And so I sat on our deck (or looked out of the windows in deference to the hot and humid St. Louis summers) and reflected. One association during this period has proved particularly propitious, offering opportunities to make these reflections public. For ten years I served as editor of the St. Louis Psychological Association's monthly newsletter. This provided a platform, in the form of the back inside page, which I have continued to use to this day.

Most of the material in this book has first appeared in the pages of that newsletter, which I have used to reflect on myself, my family, my work and my world. These columns have been shamelessly self-referential, but I have come to understand that I can only understand my world by filtering it through my understanding of myself.

In the process, naturally, I *have* come to understand myself, my family, my work and my world more fully. On reflection, it seems to me that these pages are filled with a passion that I did not always recognize at the time of writing. One of the welcome developments of this exercise has been coming to appreciate that part of myself.

Here, then, are Reflections from one man's life.
Hopefully, they will prove useful to others who leaf through the pages.

Family Lessons

Discovering "Family"

Considering my beginnings as an only child, I had acquired a sizable family by fifty. There was an ex-wife and our three children, to which I had added a second wife and her twins. My five children were beginning to bring daughters- (and sons) in-law; and a half-dozen grandchildren were added to the mix.

Then there were my parents and an assorted cast of current and former in-laws and extended family members. My (adopted) father even added a long-lost daughter and her family.

It was too bad that I had so little idea what to do with them.

I grew up in an isolated farm family. I need to be clear about this, because it helps explain why I knew so little about being part of a family, and why family has become so important to me. My step-father, who later adopted me, was an angry, brooding man who -- despite being able to be superficially social -- chose to isolate himself and us. My mother, uncomfortable around others, the product of parents who themselves cut away from their families, willingly acceded to a solitary farm life.

In this context I grew up anxious, alone, and socially inept. There was school, of course, and some few friends and teachers with whom I was able to connect, but I knew nothing of their *families*. Until high school -- really, until my first marriage -- I knew virtually nothing about how any other families operated.

Mine hardly operated at all. Oh, we did all the essential things, working (farm life was difficult and demanding), cooking and eating and cleaning, and sitting around in the evening; but we never did anything *together*. Any conversation was strictly functional ("Pass the salt;" "Don't forget to put your boots on;" "I'm going out to the barn"); no one ever really said anything *personal*, no one *shared*, and certainly no one ever *listened*.

So when I made my escape to college (thank God for good grades!) I had a lot more to learn than math and science. Unfortunately, what I needed to know was not taught in any of the courses I wandered into, and to a very real (and unfortunate) extent I have used my wives and their families for "in-service training." I owe them more thanks for this than I can ever find a way to communicate.

I was approaching 45, and a dozen years into a college teaching career, when the handwriting on the wall became clear: I was an unlikely candidate for tenure. Despite working hard -- perhaps *too* hard -- I was doing all the wrong things. While I was worrying about teaching and students and community service, and even directing grant-funded applied research, I was *not* writing books or learned articles for professional journals. The only future I was likely to have in the university was as an administrative hack.

But I did have a doctorate in psychology so, at the suggestion of a friend, I approached the university's counseling center director and worked out an informal internship. It was the best vocational move I have ever made; I was able to use two years at the counseling center to secure self-awareness, counseling experience, and the credentials for licensure.

And so I was 46 years old when I ventured out of the University's ivy-covered counseling offices and set up an office in the "real world." It took less than two weeks for me to realize that I had absolutely no idea what I was doing.

At the University I had been counseling individuals. We talked about families and relationships, of course, but my immediate focus was the individual in the office with me. The private-practice group I joined was sending me couples and families. I did not have the foggiest idea what to do with them. Not only did I have no way to understand what was going on with the couples and families unfortunate enough to be in my office, I was too consumed by feelings of inadequacy, and too reactive to the problems they brought, to use the skills that I did possess.

So when a flyer from the local Mental Health Association, announcing a six-session "Introduction to Family Therapy" workshop, crossed my desk I jumped. It was the second best move I ever made, introducing me to a whole new world -- or, more accurately, a whole new way to look at the world. For the first time I began to understand "family" as a complex interactive system, one that responds *over there* when it is pushed *over here*. For the first time my own experiences, in my own families, began to make sense.

I followed the six-week program with a two-year post-graduate certificate program in marriage and family therapy at Washington University in St. Louis; with avid reading; and with as many continuing education workshops as I could find. I worked hard at trying to apply the concepts I was learning to the couples and families (and individuals, who, of course, were parts of families) I was seeing. And, mostly, I struggled to understand and apply the concepts to myself and my own family.

And so it came to be that, approaching fifty, I finally began to make some sense out of what "family" might mean, what a family could be, and -- most importantly of all -- how *I* could be a part of it.

Miracles can happen. But sometimes they take a long time.

Coming to Terms with Mom and Dad

The Cat Woman of Golden City
(March, 1989)

I grew up with the birds.

It began, I think, when my mother, then a young city girl isolated on a primitive mid-Missouri farm, "rescued" a baby Baltimore oriole that had blown out of its nest. After experimenting with various foods (such as bread soaked in milk; as far as I know she did not dig worms) she found a way to raise it. One thing led to another, and in a few years she was seriously raising canaries and parakeets.

We lived in a two-story house, with four upstairs rooms. Three of the upstairs rooms were filled with birds: one with canaries in cages and two with parakeets flying loose. The fourth room, between two rooms of parakeets, was mine. In fact, my mother had to go through my room to get to the canaries and one room of parakeets.

The effect of this placement was significant, if not entirely clear. There was the ever-present smell, of course, and constant chirping. There was my constantly getting in trouble for frightening the birds by such innocuous behaviors as bouncing a rubber ball against our common wall. And there were the flying lessons.

One might expect that parakeets are born knowing how to fly, and, in fact, I suppose they are. Apparently, however, intricacies such as *turning* and *braking* must be learned -- the hard way. All day and night young parakeets could be heard practicing their lessons: *flutter - flutter - flutter - splat* (into the wall) *plop* (onto the floor); *flutter - flutter - flutter - splat* . . . .

Mom stopped raising birds when people in Florida discovered that they could raise large numbers of parakeets in outdoor cages and the bottom fell out of the bird market. Now, somewhat paradoxically, she's into cats.

Not raising them – just owning, feeding, and observing them. News, to Mom, is about cats. If she sends pictures, they are of cats. Now, understand: she lives in a small rural town of some 900 mostly retired people, where a "happening" is someone scheduling an appointment with the doctor. And yet, I can't help wondering. . . .

We visited Mom last weekend. Considering her age, she is doing well; and so are Callie and MJ, her two cats (considering *their* ages). When we walked down to the local grocery – flea market Mom took along a container of cat food. She directed us to an area behind the store where she walked over to some aluminum pie pans near the store's rear door.

Cats came from all directions: small ones, big ones, black cats, a white cat, two calico cats, pregnant cats . . . nine in all, I think. They came from under buildings, around corners, literally from nowhere. For hungry animals, however, they were surprisingly polite and respectful. Mom does this, I understand, once or twice a week, as often as her health and the weather permit.

I don't know what the cats mean to my mother, but I do understand that they are metaphors. I also understand that metaphors, ultimately, are personal. *I* saw homeless cats, and an aging woman who cared about them.

Since returning home two things have occurred to me about the experience. The first is *how* she cares: my mother shows love by taking care of, by fixing, by (as my chronic weight problem may attest) feeding. It's not anything I did not know, but it is a useful reaffirmation.

The second observation has to do with metaphor: homeless cats bring to mind broader problems, such as homeless people. Tens of thousands of persons live each day on the streets, or in abandoned buildings and shelters, deprived of the things the rest of us take for granted: addresses, food, jobs, healthcare, or even hope.

Measured against our national efforts to protect the economic interests of the affluent they are a national embarrassment, pushed out of sight so that you and I will not experience guilt. Individually, it seems, there is little any of us can do. As a psychologist in private practice I cannot even offer homeless persons much in the way of mental health services.

But we must not allow this problem to fade from view. We must look for what we may be able to do, and we must insist that the problem be acknowledged.

It is the least we can do. Perhaps it is a lesson we can learn from an old lady going out of her way to feed a small town's homeless cats.

The Nursing Home
(September, 1992)

The man and his wife drove silently late into the night before finding an ancient motel with a vacancy that, surprisingly, delivered as advertised a "large, clean, quiet room." Their silence was in part because it was a Friday, the end of a difficult week for each of them; but also because of the purpose of the trip: to move the man's father into a nursing home.

The previous weekend the man's mother, who had stoically nursed her husband through more than four years as his cancer and emphysema worsened, finally acknowledged that she could "no longer handle it." He was becoming increasingly irrational, she said; forgetful; and he complained about increased pain. She was "exhausted." But she was afraid that he would refuse to go "into a home;" and so the man and his wife were making the trip to give his mother support, and to assure his father that the move was necessary.

The difficult decision to move a parent into a nursing home has become common for middle-aged adult children. Improved medical care and increased life span have resulted in parents living longer. Aging parents who have been responsible for families all their lives do not easily relinquish the illusion that they can care for themselves. It is an understandable, perhaps natural, desire to complete one's life in the security of a place that has been home. At the same time today's economic and social realities have created primary family models where there is only one adult, or where both adults work. As a result, there is too often no one at home to provide needed care.

But economic and social realities change more rapidly than social and cultural expectations; and so the "placement decision" continues to be filled with doubt, uncertainty and guilt. One may feel that he or she is being unfaithful, abandoning the very person that gave them life. Or he or she may resent being responsible for an aging parent remembered as abusive, neglectful, or intrusive. Whatever the reason, it may be impossible to consider the end of one's parents' lives without also encountering unresolved family-of-origin relationship issues.

Although the man was initially shocked to see how frail and weak his father had become, he also realized that the old man was cogent, aware, surprisingly alert. It became readily apparent, however, that his mother indeed could not cope. She had always handled her anxieties by working, and in recent years her "work" was nursing her husband. As he became more housebound and bedfast, unfortunately, he had no longer been able to "manage" their systemic anxiety by "getting away:" going outside, walking the two blocks "to town," or just going into another room for a nap.

While the man's mother did not realize what was happening, his father did. When they were finally alone he told his son he knew he would "have to go to a home" so "she can calm down."

Moving into a nursing home carries an inevitable sense of finality. One goes there because he or she needs personal or nursing care; and the halls and rooms are filled with others in similar straits. There is a sadness there: even the best homes seem filled with old and lonely people, no longer needed or wanted. Much more than hospitals today, the nursing home seems to be the place one goes to die. While necessary, and increasingly inevitable, it is not an institution with which society finds comfort.

The man stood beside his father's bed an hour or two after they had arrived at the home. Necessary paperwork had been completed; and the old man was tired from the trip, which he had insisted be made in the son's car. The rest of the family, the man's wife and his mother, had already started down the hall to leave.

The man held his father's hand and told him that they were leaving, and that he and his wife would return to the city the next day. He said he would be back to see him as soon as possible.

The old man understood both the spoken and unspoken parts of the message. "You're leaving? Have a good trip. Take care of yourselves." And the old man, who had lived his life without tears, began to cry.

The younger man, who earned his living encouraging others to share their feelings, hesitated a moment. He then released his father's hand, turned, and walked away.

The Old Man's Name
(December, 1992)

I received his name formally when I was 16. My stepfather approached me with the idea of adoption, saying he had wanted to wait until "I was old enough to make my own decision."

At the time I recall primarily feeling anger. We did not have a particularly good relationship. He was not an easy person to live with, and I was "holding on" until I could leave home for college. Furthermore, I could see no "decision" to be made: "no" really wasn't an option. I would have preferred their having handled the adoption when I was younger, when there was no illusion of participation.

The question of the name itself never even occurred to me. I had used his name as far back as I could remember, having been registered as "Scott" when I first went to school. I suppose my mother and he did not want to "explain" to other people in mid-1940s rural Missouri. Perhaps they insisted that they had "lost" my birth certificate.

The relationship difficulties had also been there as long as I could remember, and continued through the years. My sense of the "differences" between us was vivid, and I always felt that I disappointed him. He was tough, a brawler; I was timid, convinced I was a coward. He was uneducated (although looking back, I now realize that he was very bright); I was a reader, most accomplished in school. He was a farmer who enjoyed nothing more than fishing; I suffered from severe allergies and hated being outdoors.

I recognize now that I was quite mistaken about his impression of me: what I had perceived as his disdain of my abilities was probably intimidation. Only in recent years have I come to understand how much my mother, struggling with her own emotional needs, had triangulated the two of us, enmeshing me in a coalition with her in which he, my stepfather, was the "bad guy." I saw him as angry (which he certainly was); dangerous (which was an exaggeration); and anti-social (which was not true at all).

For twenty years or more I handled these relationship problems through avoidance, staying away, seldom calling or writing, dealing only with my mother when there was contact. Living two years in Texas, ten years in California, and four years in Virginia made that strategy easier; but I would have done the same thing living in the same town.

For the past dozen years or so, however, I have realized that I have needed to "make my peace" with him; and, in spite of constantly finding my mother in the way had gradually made some progress.

When he was diagnosed four years ago with cancer the issues came more clearly into focus. Over the past year, as his condition worsened, the need to know about him, about his life, intensified. My efforts were of limited success: as he became frail he could sustain little conversation; and there was always my mother, in the way, obsessed with nursing him.

The call came early on a recent Saturday morning. Although there was the inevitable uncertainty, I decided to drive across the state to the nursing home we had taken him to a few weeks earlier. I arrived at the home about 5:30. The old man appeared in a coma, breathing labored. I briefly touched his hand. Planning to stay the night, I turned to arranging my mother's trip home. It was not necessary. The old man quietly died at 5:50.

Even in death I found it hard to spend time with him. Mother needed support. There were relatives to call. There were arrangements to make. The brief moments alone were much like such moments had always been: too much to say, no words to say them.

Only later, weeks later, as time passes and defenses ease do some of the thoughts become clearer. Only later can I begin to acknowledge how intertwined my identity has been with him. Much of what I am (and what I am not) has been defined by what he was. Glimmers of understanding begin to shape themselves into a sense of being. It is only a beginning; but it is time to begin.

One of the first recognition is that I have carried his name for more than half a century. It is how I am known; it is who I am. It has been, and is, a good name.

This is one of the things I would have said, if I had known the words, if there had been a way:

"Thanks for the name, Dad."

Roadway Angst and Old Folks' Paranoia
(June, 1998)

I tried to drive into the rear seat of a Suzuki 4X4 the other day. Since I was going very slowly (about 3 miles per hour) damage was slight: a broken tail light and a few scratches on the Suzuki, and about $1500 for my Honda.

The disparity resulted from the encounter of my Honda's hood with the Suzuki's spare tire, perfectly located hood-high on its backside. In addition to adding another plank in my anti-SUV platform, the incident has gotten me thinking, of all things, about growing older.

Don't tell my insurance company, but the accident was pretty much my fault. I was following the Suzuki turning right, on my way, ironically, to the dentist. After the Suzuki's driver accelerated to join traffic I inched forward, watching oncoming traffic, and proceeded through the turn with a later opening.

Well -- *partly* through the turn: the Suzuki's driver had stopped, waiting for the same car that I was watching to pass. Who would have thought that a guy who looked like a short Mark McGwire, with a cigar clamped between his teeth, driving a beat-up Suzuki, would be so cautious?

The encounter with the Suzuki has exacerbated for me a growing sense of roadway angst. In part this is because of the proliferation of high-silhouette vehicles on the highways; but I fear that it may also be because I am, alas, feeling old. I had, after all, just returned from a Mother's Day weekend trip to western Missouri to take my mother to the doctor. At 79 she is decreasingly capable of self-care and increasingly frightened about the world around her. I'm afraid I may not be far behind.

As to the first issue, it seems to me that two out of every three vehicles on I-44 (an unscientific survey, to be sure, and probably biased) are tractor-trailers, vans or mini-vans, pick-up trucks, or sports utility vehicles. A driver (especially an aging and stressed-out driver!) in an ordinary sedan has little or no visibility -- either to see what is ahead or, more fearfully, to be seen by other drivers who's lines of sight pass well above his roof. Fears of becoming a Honda ham in an oversized road hog sandwich seem less irrational every time we make the trip.

There have been small signs, recently, that my mother has been slipping: reports that she is constantly tired, memory lapses, repeated stories (even in a single conversation), and increasing anxieties. There have also been more ominous signs: concerned telephone calls from neighbors, reports of falling in the house, and a particularly disturbing incident where she fell onto a neighbor's couch and could not get up for several minutes. Finally, just before Mother's day, a fall on the way to church badly injured her leg.

And so my wife and I took my mother to see her doctor, a rather cavalier man who treats "no news" (of problems) as "good news." Her yelp of pain when he squeezed her swollen leg did get his attention, as did my (repeated) expressions of concern about possible "TIAs" (mini-strokes). But he never did "get" my concern about her increasing agoraphobia.

When the doctor suggested that she stay in the hospital for a few days to assess the possibility of TIAs she protested vehemently. Who would take care of her cat? How would she get home? Somehow, it never seems to occur to her that I -- her only child -- would be there for her.

Later that day Marilyn and I raised the possibility of her (with the cat) moving into an apartment (or assisted living) in St. Louis, so we could be more accessible than the current six-hour drive. After appearing to consider the idea briefly all her (formidable) powers of resistance were activated. We have since heard, from several of her friends, that she will "*not,* under any circumstances," let me move her to St. Louis.

My mother does not realize this, but *I do* understand her fear. I am not that far, myself, from the time when one of my well-meaning (but obviously misguided!) children will want me to move into their home, or -- worse yet -- *a home*, for my own "comfort and care." What makes me think I will be any more accepting?

As our society ages we face these problems of "old folks' paranoia" more and more. I hope we have found better solutions by the time I get there.

Although I'm afraid we may not have all that much time.

Mother's Day
(June, 1999)

This is a difficult story to write, and may be difficult for many of you to read.

Saturday of Mother's Day weekend began when Marilyn, who had gotten out of the car for a pit stop, sat on the sunglasses I had left on her seat. It ended with my smashing three fingers in the articulated section of an overhead garage door. If anything, it was worse in between.

My mother has – had -- fleas. While I realize this line has comic effect the condition – the flea infestation brought on by her bringing two stray cats into the house – was no laughing matter. I had come home from a visit with her two weekends earlier with at least a dozen bites; and the related problems – odor, scratches, disease and, with her poor vision, the possibility of being tripped and hurt – were quite serious.

So when Darlene, whom we have hired (largely against mother's wishes) to help her continue to live independently, called to describe the worsening situation I realized I had to respond. There is nobody else, one of many consequences of being an only child.

I asked Marilyn to come with me because I realized, as I thought through all that had to be done, that I could not do it myself. We had to arrange spraying, of course; but needed to vacuum first. The "adopted" stray cats needed to be taken to a veterinarian to be dipped and, if she was going to continue to take responsibility for them, spayed and neutered. All her bedding and throw rugs – she had dozens – had to be laundered. And Mother, whose developing dementia has intensified an ever-present oppositional nature, had to be managed through it all.

I learned Friday morning about the kittens. We knew one of the cats had been pregnant, of course, and (since she suddenly was thinner) must have delivered. But there was no sign of kittens until Friday. It turned out that there were five, three weeks old and cute as could be. But what would an 80-year-old woman with developing dementia do with *seven* cats?

So I was distracted Saturday morning as we drove the last half of the 300 miles to Mother's little town (probably the only environment in which she could maintain any form of independence). And I was angry, which explains snapping at Marilyn after she demolished my glasses and, on arriving at Mother's, screaming at an 80-year-old senile woman who wanted to "forget the whole thing."

"No! We are not going to forget anything! Since you insisted on letting those cats in the house, you have to deal with the results!"

Hands on hips, Mother rose to her full five-foot-one: "Is this the way you treat your patients?" It was an amazingly lucid moment. Nor knowing whether to strangle her or laugh, I could only walk away.

There were hours of vacuuming and cleaning, 14 loads of laundry, seven cats to be captured and transported and – perhaps most difficult – instructions to be given to the vet to "dispose of the kittens." Returning home after repeatedly admonishing Mother not to put cat food out (thus attracting more stray cats and more fleas), Marilyn and I walked the two blocks to "Cookies," a surprisingly good local restaurant. Less than an hour later, on our return, we found a can of cat food beside the back door.

Little wonder that my fingers were in the garage door as I slammed it shut.

The problem of what to do with aging parents, of how to discern and handle that point at which they are no longer capable of independent living, has become one of the most vexing consequences of longer life expectancy, exacerbated by whatever unresolved issues remain between adult child and parent.

Where the decline is abrupt (or awareness of the decline is sudden) the decision may be easier. But when the decline is slow, and particularly when the parent remains active and the decline is cognitive, finding the right point, figuring out what to do, is particularly difficult. And in a culture where most adults work outside the home, where little extended family support is available, choices often become excruciating.

We have elected to support Mother's remaining independent as long as possible, recognizing that in so doing we are increasing the likelihood of catastrophe. In part we have chosen this route because of an (untestable) judgement that her growing obsessiveness and agoraphobia would not allow her to survive a forced move. But there are no assured answers, no "right" choices.

Just, unfortunately, best guesses with very real consequences.

For Mary, Whom I Did Not Know
(June, 2002)

When I stopped in at the nursing home to see Mother the other day she was sitting in the day room holding a fur-covered doll. I recognized the doll, having first seen it a year earlier when we moved Mom to the downstairs "Special Needs Unit" after a series of attempts to run away.

As Kathy, the head nurse, showed us around the unit last year, she introduced us to Mary M., who would become Mom's roommate. Mary, who had apparently lost the ability to speak, was holding the doll, the very picture of motherly love. Occasionally, during the first few months in the unit, Mom would be found with Mary's doll, apparently thinking it was hers.

But Mom had lost much of her mobility recently, especially after a bad fall on the first-floor patio, and she has ceased wandering about, picking up loose objects. So I was a little surprised to see her with the furry doll, which I identified as "Mary's." Mom looked a bit confused, but that has been a common expression recently. Still, I began to wonder when Kathy commented that Mary had "left" the doll for Mom.

Hesitating, I walked to Mom's room. Sure enough, the second bed in the room was stripped. Mary, I learned, had died a few days earlier.

Nursing homes are microcosms of life, albeit primarily the last stages of life, and therefore present residents, staff and visitors with a full range of life-emotions. There are moments of excitement, brought about because of accomplishment, such as the husband who excitedly reported recently that his stroke-disabled wife had identified him as her "dear husband." There are moments of poignancy: an elderly couple, sitting in the lobby, holding hands. And there are many moments of anguish, moans and cries of distress: "Would you help me please?"

But mostly, nursing homes, like life itself, are about loss, again and again eliciting feelings of grief. Mom entered the home a little over a year ago aware enough of her surroundings to repeatedly act out her commitment to "walk all the way home." Now she seems to have no sense of place at all. In the beginning, she drew on her memories of having been a nurse to talk about other residents as if she were working, on staff; now she apparently has no memories of ever having been a nurse.

A year ago, Mom worried about Mary, who "sleeps in the room I sleep in," because she "never says a word." We noted, however, that that did not mean that Mary was unaware: in fact, she followed our movements about the room with expressive eyes. As we became more comfortable with her in the room she became a *presence*, accepting and approving.

Despite Mom's sharing a room with Mary for more than a year we learned little about her. Pictures of family members, including a granddaughter who looked a lot like her, adorned her side of the room. A daughter lived nearby, must have come weekly, and did her laundry. I once met a son, who lived in Arizona.

Our only significant interaction with Mary occurred this February, at Mom's birthday "party." She had been on the Special Needs Unit for about a year, and we had become familiar with many of the residents. We brought a small cake, and Mom, aware that she was the center of attention, seemed to enjoy herself. I occupied myself cutting pieces of cake for other residents and feeding Mom, while Marilyn took pieces to others in the day room.

When she came to Mary she realized that she would have to slowly give her very small bites. As she did so, I watched from across the room. Mary followed Marilyn's every movement with her eyes, appreciation and pleasure evident. When she had taken the last piece she looked at Marilyn and mouthed the words, "Thank you." It could only be described as a "holy moment."

I left the nursing home soon after learning of Mary's death, struggling with waves of sadness. A few blocks down the road, in the privacy of my car, I began to cry. These were tears, I knew, for many losses: for Mother, who is no more who she once was; for myself, who would never be able to give to her the joys I have always wished for her; for the endless life-losses encountered at every turn in every nursing home. . . .

And for Mary, whom I did not know.

Homecoming
(June, 2004)

When the possibility of coming to St. Louis was first raised, as the indicators of dementia increased, she was opposed, telling friends that "there was no way" she would ever let her son take her there. "Even if he tries," she vowed, "I'll come back home." Because she lived in a small town with many neighbors to look out for her, her son elected to leave her in her own home as long as possible.

But Golden City is a long way from St. Louis, and the time finally came -- after a series of disasters raised neighbors' concerns -- when it became clear she could no longer live alone. Still she resisted. When she realized what was happening on that fateful day her son had her hospitalized, she pulled herself to her full five-foot height and, glaring fiercely, said, "Let's don't and say we did!"

And even in the confusion of deepening dementia, with the dislocation of being transported across the state to a big, fearful city and a big, fearful nursing home, she retained enough wits to hold on to her intention to return home. Each day she would tell her son how, the night before, she had "walked all the way home," describing in detail how she had walked along the highway, stepping off when big trucks came by, until she'd finally gotten to Golden City.

Whether the stories were dreams or delusions was never clear, but they persisted. Finally, on a cold February afternoon a few weeks after her arrival, she found a way off the (locked) Alzheimer's ward, hurried down five flights of stairs, and slipped out a back door. How long she walked is unclear. Local police had received a report of "an elderly woman wearing only a sweater," but they could not find her. Finally, she found them, walking into suburban police station nearly a mile from the nursing home.

When her son talked with her about her escapade she was confused, but she did acknowledge being afraid. And she never again told him about trying to walk home.

She was moved to a special needs unit in an older part of the home where, with the help of a caring group of nurses, aids and activity workers, and in the face of continuing cognitive and physical decline, she "settled in." Over the succeeding four years, even after being moved back to the Alzheimer's unit, she became something of a fixture in the home, well known and liked.

Regular caretakers dressed her nicely, lovingly braiding her flowing white hair. When her son or daughter-in-law pushed her wheelchair around the nursing home, down to activities to see the cats, fish and rabbits, or outside for some fresh air, everyone spoke to her: "Hey, Gert!" "Gertie! How are you today?"

Alzheimer's is a terrible disease, carrying it's victims to places from which they cannot be reached, cannot reach out. Eventually, it robs their very bodies of the memory of sustaining life. When the end finally comes, it is a relief, a blessing.

Over the years, when she could still remember, Mother had often told of the time she had almost died while having a pacemaker installed. She would describe in detail how she moved toward a white light, and how she saw her mother, sister, and other relatives waiting, beckoning to her. When she described being "pulled back," brought back to life by the surgical staff, she always said she "did not want to return."

By the week after Mother's Day it became apparent that the end was near. She had stopped eating, and systems had begun to fail; and she lay in bed largely unresponsive. Hospice was engaged. On Tuesday, May 18th, when the call came that she had worsened, we were already on our way to the nursing home.

Over her final hour, as we sat beside her bed holding her hand and stroking her hair, I recalled the white-light story. "It's all right, Mom," I said. "We're here. When you're ready, you can finish that trip to the light." A few moments later, she did.

According to her wishes, Mom was laid to rest on Friday, May 21st, beside her husband of fifty years, in Golden City. Her simple graveside service, led by grandson Bob, was attended by several other grandchildren, friends from Golden City, and Marilyn and me.

There were tears and memories and hugs, exactly as she would have wanted.

And so it was that, in the fullness of time, at the end of her days, Gertrude Scott finally returned home.

Parenting, For Better or Worse

On Mountains, Yachts and Origami
(May, 1989)

Stephanie moved to Los Angeles last August to attend California State University at Northridge. Officially, she was seeking a four-year deaf communications program (she has been interested in sign language since taking an introductory course at church when she was ten). In truth, I suspect, she was seeking a more comfortable life-style.

She has established residency and appears set on staying in California. Stephanie will be 21 this year, and (with her twin brother Steve) is our youngest.

We visited her last month. She's doing fine academically and is involved on campus. We were able to meet a number of her friends -- an interesting and diverse group. While in Southern California we also visited favorite cousins of mine who live in Orange County. They have done well in life, despite the struggles that beset us all: he is a physicist working on "star wars" research and she is a program analyst for county government. They have a beautiful home, two lovely married daughters, a grandchild, and a 35-foot motorized sailboat.

Stephanie has a friend, a Japanese daughter of a businessman who brings Japanese children to this country for visits, to study, or to learn English. Marilyn and I spent a night at a campsite in the mountains, overlooking Santa Monica and the Pacific Ocean, with 51 Japanese children and several Japanese sponsors. They spoke little English and we spoke no Japanese. The only word we could agree on was "hello," accompanied each time with a bow. It was a delightful experience.

Three incidents during our stay seem to symbolize the paradox of Southern California. The first was our visit to the yacht club in Newport Beach where my cousins' boat is moored. Yacht clubs, at the very least, reflect affluence. Added to the scene of magnificent half-million dollar homes overlooking the Pacific, the picture of economic success was clear.

The second event was a side trip I took, driving between Orange County and the San Fernando Valley, through south-central Los Angeles to show a somewhat reluctant Marilyn the areas I had known during the 1965 Watts riots. Here were all the trappings of poverty: boarded buildings, old cars, and kids standing on street corners. It seemed little changed in 25 years.

And then there was our dinner at the Japanese language camp, which concluded with a dual-language orientation for the first-night students complete with the usual welcomes, rules, and bad jokes. During the proceedings one table of boys idly practiced origami, the ancient Japanese art of paper folding, with their napkins. When the meeting was over they left, leaving their paper creations behind. It was fascinating to see the American visitors scrambling for treasures the Japanese kids thought of as "doodles."

There are lessons here, I think. As I gaze at the paper napkin stork on my desk, created by a bored Japanese ten-year-old, I am reminded of a daughter who is no longer as much a part of our lives as she was. Like the kids from Japan, she is beginning something new; and her beginnings are our losses.

I think also of the struggling souls of south-central Los Angeles, still awash in hopelessness after all these years. Poverty and prejudice seem to never go out of style. And I think of the yachts and mansions of Newport Beach: as big as they are, they are still as insignificant against the vastness of the ocean as a tossed-aside folded-paper bird.

Yet even amid losses, hopelessness and insignificance there may be possibilities. Watts, after all, has its beautiful Watts Towers. And there is always the chance that we may stumble upon a bit of origami.

Uncle Dad and the Blended Wedding

(February, 1992)

Greg, 24, was the youngest from my first marriage, and was the last to marry. Curiously, Greg was marrying his sister-in-law: that is, his fiancé was the sister of his older brother's wife. Life is sometimes confusing.

Weddings, like other family life cycle events, provide opportunities for reflection. It was easy to remember Gregory as an infant: born when I was nearing 30, he came as I was beginning to break free from childhood bonds, to experience new feelings. My attachment was intensified by the infant's surgery, for pyloric stenosis, at two weeks; I can still vividly recall images of the tiny baby in the huge crib tied to wires and tubes.

Other images are less clear. Greg was barely two when his mother and I separated; and subsequent contact was sporadic, dominated by the older children, strained through confusions of anguish, guilt and pain. Greg was a quiet child, preferring to remain in the shadow of his older siblings. I can painfully recall learning, when Greg was graduating from high school, that he had always had trouble reading. Greg had never commented on the stacks of books I had given him as presents over the years.

It was not that we were not important to each other: I knew Greg loved me. It was that we did not *know* each other. It was part of the common experience of being a non-custodial parent, which I have come to call being an "uncle-dad." Non-custodial parents do not really function as parents. They operate within confused boundaries, with mixed messages, with limited and unclear authority. They move only on the perimeters of their children's realities.

Uncle-dads do not quite belong, have no obvious place in families trying to hold on to traditional "nuclear" models. I can remember earlier weddings, such as at my oldest son's wedding seven years ago, where my presence created anxiety and confusion (and I was not told I could stand in the receiving line until after the wedding); or how, when I refused to "be understanding" and let daughter Anne be "given away" by her step-father, she changed her whole wedding, holding it in a park so neither of us could do it.

Time (and events) heal; and I was much more included in Greg's wedding events. But I still felt like an outsider, "looking in" through the rehearsal and rehearsal dinner (even if I did pay for half of the dinner), and through the wedding and reception. But it was a beautiful wedding; and Greg and his bride seemed very happy, if a little bewildered and exhausted. It was good to be part of their joy.

I looked forward to getting to know new daughter-in-law Robin. But regular visits are difficult: both Greg's mother and Robin's family live in Marion, Illinois, some 150 miles away; and holiday priorities are always to go there. It is always possible to join them there, of course; but there are other family commitments, and I'd still be an outsider.

Still uncle-dad, after all these years. One of the realities of today's blended families.

How Can I Know Thee?
(August, 1992)

The first time I saw Stephanie she was a little over one year old, sitting with her twin brother Stephen on the floor of her mother's home in Anna, Illinois. I remember the scene as if it were yesterday: Stephen immediately crawled into my lap, while Stephanie, ever wary, sat back, watching and waiting.

It was a pattern often repeated. After their mother and I married (when they were four), Steve quickly came to call me "daddy." Stephanie resisted, not publicly bestowing paternal status until pressured into doing so by playmates nearly two years later.

But in a surprising way, considering my insecurities at the time, I understood. I was, I realized, the only father figure Stephen and Stephanie knew. And I also knew how much I needed them: to the extent that I could be a father to them, I could assuage some of my guilt for not being with my own children, for not seeing them enough.

And so I *wanted* to be a good father (or, as I gradually came to understand the difference, stepfather), even though my *performance* never lived up to my self-imposed demands. And I suppose, looking back over the years, like most of us, I was all right as a parent: I did some things well, some things acceptably, and some things pretty abysmally.

Stephanie and Stephen are 24 now. Steve graduated from Southwest Missouri State last year and, like so many others of his age, is still looking for a job in his field of choice, television production. Marilyn and I attended Stephanie's graduation, from California State University at Northridge, the end of May.

It is easy to feel proud of Stephanie. She enrolled at Northridge because of its' nationally known program in American Sign Language interpreting for the deaf, an interest she developed as a child in church. She graduated *cum laude*, honored as the "deaf studies student of the year." From the shy child of her youth, she has blossomed into a confident, attractive, active young lady; compassionate, committed, a California campus activist.

Watching the graduation under a broiling late afternoon San Fernando Valley sun I realized how proud I was of Stephanie, and, despite being "only a stepparent," how proud I was of qualities of mine she may have incorporated. But there was a bittersweet quality to these reflections: I also realized, watching her at her graduation and during the events of the weekend, that after all these years, despite all my love, I really do not know her as much as I would like.

Perhaps it is always this way. Perhaps, as parents, we can never really know our children. Perhaps we have no way of knowing anyone else, really, no matter how much we love them, except through our own eyes – that is, in relation to what we know about ourselves. If so, perhaps the only way we can ever really know our children is to the extent they show us ourselves (or mirror images of ourselves).

This may be, for all I know, yet another limitation in being a stepparent: a child cannot show biology he or she does not share. Or perhaps the problem is within me, to the extent that I grew up disconnected, and to the extent that I continue, despite efforts, desires and wishful thinking, to function in disconnected ways. After all, if we wish to *know* another, we must allow ourselves to *be known.*

I have been Stephanie's father for over 20 years, and I love her very much. Over the years, I have come to know a lot about her, about the things she has struggles with, and about the things she cares about. I like what I know very much. But I know there is much I do not know, perhaps can never know.

I still cannot shake the image of the little girl, sitting back on her haunches, watching, waiting. Or of the four year old, holding back on saying "daddy." I wonder, sometimes, what she was waiting for. I wonder, sometimes, if she is still waiting.

I keep thinking that she may be waiting for me.

Sons and Fathers
(November, 1992)

In the end, the most meaningful event of the weekend happened in the men's room.

"The weekend" was the 2nd International Men's Conference in Austin, Texas, a three-day "gathering of men" that featured speakers of varying renown (including Sam Keen, Warren Farrell, and Herb Goldberg), workshops of varying relevance, and opportunities of varying significance.

The event was somewhat misnamed: it was not really international in scope or size (only two or three hundred participants, most from Texas). But the events of the weekend were typically interesting and sometimes quite powerful.

Yes, there were drums. There were drums *everywhere,* and especially in plenary sessions, which were introduced by drummers, informally organized, gradually progressing to a crescendo. Drums were used by many men to affirm points of popular agreement made by speakers or to "honor" individuals or groups. Even the "elders" were honored, the first time I have been part of a group applauded (to say nothing of being "drummed") solely because of longevity.

Individual indications of affirmation were also common, sometimes expressed quietly (**"HO!"**), and sometimes resoundingly (**"HO!"**). It was truly an Excedrin weekend.

Two workshops stand out. The first was "Exploring the Wall between Gay, Bisexual and Heterosexual Men," organized by a gay man and a heterosexual man from Austin. Participants (about 80 of us, fairly evenly divided between gay, bisexual and heterosexual men) were led through a two-hour experiential process designed to identify and confront the fears, anger and conditioning that separate us. The workshop, which began with men holding hands and parading through the hotel lobby (not an experience most of us had previously enjoyed), continued with men in each group identifying and hurling "hate epithets" at each other across a "wall," and ended with men sharing feelings, embracing, and even crying together, was powerful.

But the most affecting event for me was a workshop I decided to attend at the last minute. "Like Father, Like Son: Healing the Father-Son Relationship" was led by a father, Jack Hosman, and his son, Cal. Jack Hosman, now a therapist, was a Presbyterian minister and missionary who had been much loved by everyone except his family, whom he alternately ignored or raged against. Cal Hosman is now about 30, a teacher, and the informal "poet-laureate" of the Texas men's group.

Two minutes into Jack Hosman's account of his parenting sins (and Cal Hosman's account of their impact) I was fighting tears, recognizing myself in both men. Initially, narcissistically, I assumed I was alone in my tears; but gradually, as man after man described his own personal family-of-origin horror, the sounds of sobbing around the room became apparent.

At the time I was focused on my own experiences, trying to know – and grieve – two fathers, one dying, the other dead. Nevertheless there was some recognition, even then, that I needed – *wanted* – to initiate reconciliation with my own sons. Perhaps, I thought, I could invite them to next year's conference.

It was only later, in the solitude of a sleepless early morning that I found myself focusing on Steve. Of my three sons, Steve is the one I have "raised": Bob was eight and Greg two when their mother and I divorced. I have known Steve since he was little more than one year old; he was only four when his mother and I married. As the only real father-figure he has had I think I have provided him with a positive model of responsibility, goodness, and marital hopefulness. I *have* cared for him, supported him, and unquestionably loved him.

What I *have not* done, I am afraid, is *connect* with him: there has been too little touching, too little sharing, too little intimacy he could emulate. There has been too much distance, withholding, unclarified anger. Too painful, in the 4:00 AM silence, was the memory of times I would catch him watching me, observing what he must have perceived as a threatening mood, backing away. (As Jack and Cal Hosman observed, there is so much *isolation* in anger.)

And so it was, at 4:00 AM, alone in the darkness, that the tears finally came. Although painful, the tears also felt good. Perhaps, this time, they will not be in vain. Perhaps, this time, I will be able to show them to my sons.

After Jack and Cal's workshop I went into the men's room in the hotel lobby. Another man, who had been in the same workshop, came in. "Are you all right?" he asked as he passed toward the urinals. It was a simple question, but one borne of shared experience, of recognition and acknowledgment. I do not know the man's name, but I thank him, for he demonstrated that intimacy can be created in simple gestures, in mundane places.

And so, here's to Steve, and to Bob and Greg: I want – very much – I to connect, to break out of my isolation, to share with you and to hear from you, even to hear about the pain I have created. I want – very much – to be able to say, tearfully, unashamedly, "I love you." I know I need your help to do this; but I also recognize that it is *my* job, *my* responsibility as father, to initiate the process.

To Steve, Bob and Greg: **HO!**

Wedding Lessons
(October, 1993)

A client, beset with chronic and seemingly insoluble problems and given to depths of depression, recently observed that his "black moods" seemed to be the only "true reality" – that hopeful scenarios were "only illusions." As he talked it became clear that his black moods resulted from experiences recalling childhood feelings of hopelessness.

As a psychologist I know how easily one can re-encounter childhood realities; how accessible the child is within us. As a person struggling with life, however, I also know we create new realities, just as real as those of childhood.

We had a wedding in the family a few weeks ago. Steve, the child of my wife's that was four when we married 21 years ago, married Michele. While Steve was not my first child to be married, his was (as a friend termed it) the first "resident child's" wedding. It was, therefore, a big event, invested with hoopla, tuxedos and anxiety. It was also a beautiful weekend: spectacular weather, lovely ceremony, good times with family and friends.

They came from all directions: Steve's twin sister, Stephanie, and her friend Brian from California; two of my sons and daughters-in-law (and two grandsons) from Kansas City and Tennessee; Steve's aunt and uncle from Boston; old family friends from Illinois; as well as many friends from St. Louis. It was good to share the special event with special people.

Weddings, of course, are significant family events, major transition points in a family's life-cycle. Even in the midst of all the confusion it is only natural to reflect on the meanings of events, large and small. On the larger scale I have never been able to watch a son or daughter be married without sadness and fear, as well as joy, because I know all too well how difficult it is to learn how to live well with another person.

Steve and Michele have prepared well for their life together. They have been friends for years, engaged for two years; seem comfortable with each other and each other's friends. They seem able to be together, or apart, without anxiety. Their love appears wholesome, unpossessive. I understand too well that life presents us all with unexpected and untested trials; but I want to believe that this young couple is as ready as they can be.

But weddings are significant for everyone involved. This one, for example, confronted some of my own "realities:" raised on an isolated farm as a "lonely only," too much alone, not belonging. And so it was especially meaningful to see people at the wedding because they were *my* friends; to enjoy my wife's sister and brother-in-law as much as if they were *my* siblings; to feel a part of the "crowd" that gathered for family pictures with the bride and groom and realize that they were *my* family.

We are never far from the child within. But the realities we create are just as much a part of us. In the best of times we realize that the realities we have created are good -- very, very good.

Welcome to the family, Michele.

Absent Fathers and Grandma 'Leen
(June, 1995)

Grayson slept through most of his second birthday party. When he went to sleep there was no one at Papa Jerry's except his parents and older brother Andrew. When he awoke the house (and yard) was filled with people, many of whom he did not know. So he was somewhat subdued as Andrew directed the opening of his presents.

Grayson recognized his grandparents, of course; and that was no small feat. Altogether, including biological, step- and other "grandparent figures" Grayson could, in the words of his Presbyterian minister father, "Fill a small church." He knew "Grandma Linda," who he sees most often, well enough to climb into her lap. He knew "Grandma 'Leen" well enough to be comfortable with her as well. He does not see "Papa Ron" very often, so he avoided me during most of the festivities.

"Grandma 'Leen" is Marlene, preacher Bob's mother, so named in testimony of brother Andrew's inability, when younger, to put "grandma" and "Marlene" in the same sentence at the same time. In addition to Bob, Marlene raised younger sister Anne (now married, with four children, and living in England), and youngest brother Greg (married and living in Kansas City). Marlene had some help from stepfather Harry, especially during the difficult teen years. She did not have much help from me: Marlene and I were divorced before Bob was eight years old.

A recent Mona Charon column in the *Post-Dispatch* dealt with the problem of absent fathers. Now, I must confess to not reading Charon regularly -- somehow, a conservative female columnist seems, to me, to be an oxymoron.

Nevertheless, Charon's May 23, 1995 column entitled "Fathers, Families and Commitment," in spite of some obligatory "liberal bashing," raised important issues worth consideration. Citing data from researcher Sarah McLanahan, Charon reported that children raised by only one parent were twice as likely to drop out of high school, get pregnant before marriage, have drinking problems, or be divorced themselves than were children raised by two parents.

These are, as Charon observes, difficult findings. We (including the population of "absent fathers" in which I hold membership) would prefer to think that divorce does not matter that much, that children are resilient, that growing up in a less-conflicted single-parent home is better for children. And, of course, there are many instances in which children from broken homes grow up to be very healthy adults. For example, Bob, Anne and Greg are respectful and productive young adults.

But single-parent families are almost always economically worse off; a single parent cannot possibly provide the same level of support, attention and monitoring that two parents could provide; and children from separated/divorced families inevitably face the absence of a parent during key development periods and/or are too often "put in the middle" between feuding parents.

That children manage to survive such circumstances at all may be testimony to the fact that they *are* resilient. But it may also indicate that one or both of their parents are working hard to be good parents; and, of course, that they may have been able to grow as individuals in spite of their personal problems.

A recent airing of a Barbra Streisand concert, which contained clips of several of her movies, brought to mind *The Way We Were,* the Redford-Streisand film in which two ill-fitted individuals married, had a daughter, and ultimately divorced. In a scene near the end of the movie Hubble (played by Redford) is watching his daughter from across the street. Though trite and predictable the scene always reduces me to tears.

These observations are not meant to be about guilt or blame. My relationship with the children from my first marriage is strong today, a reflection, I suspect, to their perseverance as much as to anything I have done. But I know I missed too much of their childhood; and I am sure they missed much more. I will always be sad about that.

Time (and life's events) heals many wounds, and Marlene and I have a good relationship now. We can be comfortable at the same family gatherings; and, as far as I can tell, so can our respective spouses. I feel (and experience) a level of mutual respect and caring. I only hope she knows how much I respect and appreciate the job she did in raising three wonderful kids.

Good work, Grandma 'Leen!

A Beginning, an Ending, and a Symbol of Hope
(July, 2002)

By any accounts, our daughter Stephanie was a beautiful bride, a fact in which I take considerable pleasure but no credit, as she carries none of my genes. But I did help to raise her, becoming her step-father when she was four, so I can be proud that she has grown, at age 34, into such a responsible, caring and loving young woman (even though, I daresay, most of that credit also belongs to her mother).

The wedding, at the Old Meeting House on Geyer Road south of Clayton -- a lovely spot for a small family affair -- brought Gerry Crotty and his son Ryan into our ever-expanding family. Gerry seems to be a gentle and thoughtful man, a few years older than Stephanie (who has always been older than her years); and Ryan is delightfully full of 20-year-old assurance and angst. The family is the better for their addition.

In many ways Stephanie's wedding spoke to the possibilities of family. One of the co-officiants was her step-brother Bob; and another step-brother, Greg, and his wife Robin, flew in from Florida. In the congregation was Stephanie's father, Charlie Harris, and her step-mother, Kay, as well as her twin brother Steve and sister-in-law Michele.

Other guests – stay with me here, this gets a little complicated – included Bob's wife Linley and their children Andrew, Grayson, and newly adopted Emma Jane; Robin and Linley's mother, Linda Allen; and their father and step-mother, Jerry and Gerri Allen. Also present were my ex-wife Marlene, with her husband Harry, testimony to the healing powers of time.

And finally (am I forgetting anyone?) there was Rebecca, Steph's half-sister (Charlie's daughter), Rebecca's husband David, as well as Stephanie's niece (and flower girl) Kai, and Kai's brothers Jordan and Elijah; and Gerry's brother Art, Art's wife DeDe, and their children Robert and Annie (also a flower girl).

Yes, our understanding of "family", especially "extended family," is changing. But there is richness in the change, new textures bringing new possibilities.

The day after the wedding Stephanie and Gerry, together with Steve and Michele, drove by our old house in the Lambert Airport buyout zone of Bridgeton. After their report Marilyn and I made our own pilgrimage.

We had lived in Bridgeton for 13 years; and the twins, nine years old when we arrived, grew up there. Even with the increasingly intrusive airplane noise, it was a wonderful neighborhood in which to raise children. Now the house, purchased by the Airport Authority, is empty, stripped of anything usable, disfigured by holes smashed into walls, ready – as the blue tag on a window announces – for the bulldozer. It is as if one's life, one's very blood, sweat and tears, are rendered inconsequential.

But they were not inconsequential. The image of Stephanie, standing with her new husband Gerry in front of her brother Bob and a roomful of family members and friends, will forever testify to me the importance of those years, and the organic role a soon to be destroyed split-level on Larchburr Drive in Bridgeton played in making us a family.

Marilyn and I have been spending more time at the river lately, in our new Calhoun County home. The house is off Quarry Road; and at the bottom of that road, down-river a quarter mile or so, is, not surprisingly, a quarry. Although no longer a source of rock, the site is a repository for gravel, used locally for roads and fill.

There is a pile of gravel some fifteen or twenty feet high at the quarry, a small mountain much sought after by grandchildren seeking to prove their prowess. Grandparents, of course, do not climb gravel piles, but the quarry is a regular hiking destination, a manageable combination of distance and hills, from which we can watch the ebbs and flows of the Mississippi.

And so it was that I was struck, the other morning, as we caught our breath at the quarry, by the sight of a lone sapling, some two-thirds of the way up the eastern slope of the gravel. Here was new life, a hope-to-be tree, growing -- literally -- out of a gravel pile.

Progress may well be marked by bulldozed houses, valued only in memory; but *nature* is about survival, life, the future. There is much hope in that.

And in weddings that bring families together, in forms that are familiar as well as in forms that are new.

Generations

A Visit from Miriam
(September, 1988)

Miriam was everything you would expect for a 19 month old: energetic, imaginative, inquisitive, and as beautiful as only a first grandchild can be. She was also something of a terror: demanding, self-centered, and, like superbaby, able to trash a small house in a single bound.

A visit from a granddaughter who lives in England, who you haven't seen for over a year, should be an exciting event. But when her mother, your daughter from a first marriage, is married to an English lad, and you haven't seen them for over a year either, there are bound to be stresses: cultural differences, unresolved family issues, competitiveness between previously married parents, and miss- (or non-) communication.

It was a family theorist's dream: the air was filled with marching triangles, alliances, and coalitions. Miriam, responding to normal new-situation anxieties and (probably) subtle parental cues, refused to have anything to do with her grandfather, who, therefore, struggled with his feelings of rejection and frustration. And father and daughter also struggled with unrealistic – and therefore unmet – expectations.

It all worked out in the end. Father and daughter (and son-in-law) were able to talk through some issues. Grandfather arranged to be alone with Miriam who, after verifying there were no parents around, appeared to enjoy charming her granddad. And all three returned to England, bringing quiet and a chance to repair the house.

Miriam's Woods
(March, 1990)

I went for a walk in the woods a few days ago, remembering Miriam, and thought of identity, family, and the capacity for intimacy.

The "woods" is the span of trees that line the stream winding behind our townhouse. Miriam had taken me to a spot her mother had shown her, a spot her mother had found during a walk a few days earlier. It is a narrow expanse of trees, no more than a few hundred feet separating housing and condo developments; but to a three-year-old with her grandfather, it must have seemed like deep forest.

Miriam's spot was on a bluff overlooking the stream, where in the winter you can see across the tops of trees to houses beyond. But this was summer; and we sat on a log and shared a moment of adventure together. The next day Miriam returned to England with her mother.

Having children demonstrates the continuity of generations, allowing us to recognize our own past by seeing into the future. Experiencing grandchildren does so even more, perhaps because they come when we are not so overwhelmed with surviving, when we have matured enough to understand time beyond our own existence.

But when the grandchildren live an ocean away the opportunities to know them -- and, perhaps more importantly, for them to know us -- are much too rare. So perhaps it's reasonable for Miri's visit to lead to such profound thoughts.

Miri's short life has been stressful at times, and lived far away; so it's not surprising that a grandfather was at first just another stressor. But slowly, at the zoo, in the house, on our walks, we began to know each other. And when she walked onto the airplane for her trip home I knew we shared the sadness of parting.

Sitting in the woods the other day, gazing at the stream, I realized why Miriam's visit was so important to me, and I suspect also for her. Miriam's visit had to do with answering fundamental questions, such as "Who am I, anyway?;" with discovering one's place as part of a family, a family with pasts and futures; and with developing one's capacity for making connections with other people.

We know ourselves, in part, by knowing the past that created us; and in a very real sense we come to terms with our own identity by coming to terms with the family that produced us. And it is, hopefully, within family that we first make contact with other persons and begin to develop the skills of intimacy.

And so my walk with Miri in the woods was important for both of us. For me it was a chance to encounter a part of myself sent into the future, a bit of eternity. For Miriam it was an opportunity to experience her past; to connect with her roots, her family, and ultimately with herself. In spite of the separation there is hope in that.

So thanks for coming, Miri. I'll think of you each time I go for a walk in the woods.

Generations
(July, 1990)

The first things 21-month-old Andrew saw on entering the house late Friday evening were two black cats. A look of utter delight came to his face: eyes wide and a smile from ear to ear. His first words, "Tiddy-tat!" became a week-end mantra, repeated endlessly as he sought to achieve rapprochement with the wary cats.

Quickly recognizing that they would not sit still for his approach (in part because he was slow to learn which way to stroke their fur), and just as quickly wearing out his parents, Andrew stalked the cats with one hand firmly grasping his grandfather's finger. Grandfathers do not so quickly tire of such attentions.

Andrew's father is Bob, eldest son of his father. Bob is pastor of a Presbyterian church in Tennessee; thus, family gatherings such as this are all too infrequent. In some ways Bob is living out one of his father's early fantasies. Some would say Bob and his father, Andrew's grandfather, look alike: same beard, although Bob's is not yet gray; same tendency to paunch.

They were alike in other ways as well: the grandfather remembers well the day, admiring his son, that he realized that many of the qualities he valued in Bob were qualities he himself possessed. It was an important self-esteem milestone, demonstrating that we may learn more from our children than they from us.

Saturday, after conquering the zoo, the family sat around the table. The grandfather, keeping his own thoughts, tried to recall how his son looked at 21 months. The images were blurred, incomplete; yet somehow Andrew looked familiar. The grandfather swelled with the experience of being part of something meaningful, somehow significant. Three generations together seemed to symbolize continuity, permanence, future. Looking at Andrew, son of his son, he understood how life, although transient, continues through the ages.

Andrew discovered Katie, the neighbor's three-month-old Sheltie pup, just as he was leaving Sunday. The two hit it off instantly. Pup and child began a game of hide-and-seek, in which each intuitively understood the other's rules. On reflection it made sense: a three month old pup and a 21 month old child are developmentally about the same age. The grandfather watched, envying his grandson's ability to experience and obtain joy from his world.

We learn from our children's children as well.

Grayson
(July, 1993)

We finally met Grayson the other weekend. Grayson James Scott was born May 16th in Union City, Tennessee, the second son of Bob and Linley Scott. Bob, as careful readers of these pages may recall, is my No. 1 (as in oldest) son, and is the pastor of Trinity Presbyterian Church in nearby Martin, Tennessee. Bob and Linley's first son is Andrew, who will be five on Labor Day.

Grayson's name is significant: "James" is also my middle name. I do not know if the coincidence was intentional, but it is important to me. Grayson is, of course, a beautiful baby. Being only a few weeks old his behavioral repertoire is a bit limited, but he does suck, smack, squint, sleep, cry and make bad smells in wonderful ways.

We were the last of the grandparents to meet Grayson. Being a child of the '90s, with both parents from divorced families, Grayson has more grandparents than a small child can reasonably get to know. All the other grandparents live in Marion, Illinois (making up a sizable percentage of that town's population), so that's where most "family visits" occur.

Those who know me well will know that this – being the "last parent in line" – is something of an "issue" with me; but I think I handle it reasonably well. Marilyn and I even make pilgrimages to Marion to join in "family affairs" from time to time. Fortunately the rest of the family, including my ex-wife (most of the time) are comfortable with this.

The thing about a new grandson (or granddaughter) is that you can't meet them without encountering the *continuity of time*. There were three generations of Scott males together in Martin, representing, in all likelihood, at least a century of time; and these three generations connect with generations on end in each direction. Recognizing this lends, for me at least, new meaning to the word "eternity." Who knows what comment or act will impact a child and live through eternity as a lasting legacy?

But you can't meet a new grandchild without encountering other kinds of legacies as well. We may be populating the world with children whose progeny will live forever; but are we leaving them a world which will survive?

And so it was, driving to and from Martin, that I found myself reflecting on the news, the times, the world in which young Grayson James must make his way. I was born into a world with many problems, but I grew up with a clear sense that *life* was *valuable*. We've lost that, somehow, somewhere. We kill people -- or leave them to kill each other -- for political reasons. We have children killing children – sometimes for a jacket, sometimes for no discernible reason at all. We mobilize the police when a city's basketball, hockey or baseball team wins a championship. Violence is so commonplace it is no longer news.

And yet, we promote – and reward – ever more violent movies, television, even music. We fight with patriotic fervor any attempt to remove guns from our homes, our streets, our children. We picture on "wanted posters" people whose views or behaviors, even when legal, we do not like – and then we blame them when someone murders them.

We launch "aid missions" to starving people in other "chaotic" countries – the right things to do – but then reject minuscule, by contrast, spending programs to provide summer jobs for urban kids in our own "developed" country because they are "too costly." Somewhere, somehow, we've gotten things confused.

I recently attended a conference on "managed care." The information was overwhelming and depressing; and the implications for the future of psychology are staggering. I found relief in the thought that I am old enough to retire if things get as bad as some prophets of doom predict.

I feel the same way about the world we live in: I won't have to be around to see how bad it could get.

But then I think of Grayson.

Wind in the Tummy
(November, 1994)

We went to England a few weeks ago, but not to see the Queen. We went to see Mimi, Che', Raffi and baby Zoe, who has "wind in the tummy."

Mimi is Miriam, nearly seven, usually called Miri (except by younger brother Che' who has trouble with "r" sounds). Miri is an eldest child: most comfortable with adults, alternatively responsible for and/or bossy to her younger brothers, strong-willed, more in need of control when she is anxious. She is bright, energetic, easy to be proud of but sometimes hard to be around.

Che', on the other hand, is not a typical second child. At a little more than four Che' is beautiful, sensitive, affectionate, shy and creative. Che' experienced chronic ear infections which affected his hearing as a younger child. As a result, his speech development was delayed, lowering his self-confidence. He is easily wounded, especially by adults too busy to take the time to listen and understand. Grandparents, of course, have nothing but time, which is good because it turns out Che' has a lot to say.

Raffi (officially, Raphael) is six months past two, and is all boy: fearless, challenging, curious and constantly in motion. He approaches life with enthusiasm, whether he is climbing into the lap of a grandparent he does not know or tormenting his older brother. Watching Raffi have fun can be fun; trying to keep up can be tiring. Baby Zoe was born September 12th, less than two weeks before we arrived. She is, of course, a beautiful baby. Zoe is given to periods of colic, descriptively referred to by British "mums" as having "a bit of wind in the tummy." Everybody in the family dotes on Zoe who, her parents promise, *will* be a youngest child.

It has been three years since we had seen Miriam and Che', and we had known Raffi only *in utero.* It is difficult to keep up with grandchildren one sees regularly; almost impossible when separated by a $700 flight.

For that matter, it is also difficult to be *with* them on such infrequent visits. First, their excitement levels intensify, escalating attention-getting behaviors. Then, there are cultural and language differences: these are, after all, *English* children who speak a different version of our common tongue. Furthermore, our daughter Anne and her husband Doug are committed to a different life-style, caring little about success and the rat-race.

Perhaps because both Anne and Doug felt sometimes ignored or abandoned as children (Anne was six when my marriage to her mother ended), they have worked to create a child-friendly home, using positive structuring rather than limit-setting and criticism as much as possible. The results are strong-minded children who will try anything and who do not respond well to "no." I very much respect Anne and Doug's intent and effort, but sometimes theirs is a chaotic household.

But Miri, Che', Raffi and Zoe are *grandchildren,* fruit of my loins (Biblically speaking), and – no small credit to their parents – bright, beautiful, creative and loving. It was wonderful seeing them, both renewing old relationships and establishing new ones. They made the long flights (in cramped TWA coach), jet-lag, and obligatory bad colds (*everyone* in England is racked with coughing!) more than worthwhile. Of course, the side-trip to Ireland helped too.

By the way, although we delighted in all four kids, I was really taken by Che', perhaps because I identified most with his sensitive desire for affection. When he would say, "Well, Gwandpa Won, you know what?," I *really* wanted to know "what!"

So, here's to Miri, Che', Raffi and baby Zoe, who had "wind in the tummy." And here's to Anne and Doug, who have given us four beautiful grandchildren, and who are working hard to raise them to get as much out of life as they can.

It was a great trip!

Transforming Qiao Yu
May, 2001

Governmental attempts to address public problems through social manipulation are likely to produce unintended consequences. An example is China's attempt to reduce over-population by imposing penalties on families with more than one child. Added to long-standing cultural biases against girl babies, and the reality that only boys "pass on the family name," unintended results have included an increasingly male population (55%, by some estimates), and the abandonment of thousands of infant girls each year.

Of course, even unintended consequences have consequences. The large numbers of unwanted Chinese babies, almost all girls, provide opportunities for the ever-growing numbers of American families wanting to adopt because of infertility or other reasons.

So it was that the days-old infant girl left at the gates of a shopping mall in a small city near Changsa, the capital of Hunan Province, came to Zhuzhou Orphanage in Changsa. Named Qiao Yu (pronounced "Chow You"), she was placed on a list of babies waiting for American adoption.

With the passage of time Qiao Yu, now eight months old, was paired, administratively, with a couple from Pekin, Illinois, USA. Bob and Linley Scott, parents of two sons and wanting a daughter, had been trudging through the bureaucratic international adoption processes for more than two years when they finally learned that their "number had come up."

On April 10, 2002, Bob and Linley left St. Louis Lambert Airport for Beijing (via Los Angeles). After a few days of sightseeing they flew, with several other adopting families, to Changsa where, on Tuesday, April 16th, they met their new daughter. One day later the adoption was finalized and Qiao Yu became Emma Jane Qiao Yu Scott, the newest resident of Pekin, Illinois. To say that the new parents were thrilled would be the understatement of the year.

The trip to China for Emma Jane was, to say the least, fascinating (and exhausting) for the new parents. There were wonders to see in and around Beijing, such as the Great Wall, Ming Tombs, Forbidden City, and Summer Palace, as well as ordinary life – learning to cook Chinese dumplings and Peking Roast Duck in a Beijiner's home.

There was the "first meeting" trauma: Emma Jane cried for the first hour-and-a-half. There were strolls with the baby along the streets of Changsa, attracting much attention from Chinese youth (practicing their English) and grandmotherly women lecturing them for not dressing the baby warmly enough or too warmly.

There was also a depressing visit to the orphanage (to pay the fee and leave gifts brought from Pekin for the occasion), and even a visit to a McDonald's in Guangzhou (the third-largest city in China, from which they departed for the States), a welcome treat for Midwesterners tired of rice and chopsticks, but one that sat poorly digestively.

What is it like for an eight month old Chinese girl, after spending her entire eight months of life cared for by female Chinese caretakers, to be dropped into the arms of a strange woman and -- even worse -- a man much larger than any Chinese men she may have seen? Or to be hauled from hotel room to hotel room, from airplane to airplane, to be finally deposited in a strange city literally half-way around the earth, in the midst of a gaggle of brothers and grandparents, all competing for attention?

Emma Jane arrived at Lambert, delivered by Southwest Airline stork, on April 27th, and immediately took command. Showing no signs of the terror I would have felt, she comfortably moved from arm to arm, smiling at the funny faces, beginning the process of putting her brothers in place. By the time she left for Pekin, the next day, she had completed the process.

That Emma Jane is a beautiful baby goes without saying. What is more astounding is the ease with which she has adjusted to the changes that would, for you and me, be so difficult. It says much about the adaptability of youth.

So "Emma Jane Chow Mein" (her father's label, not mine!) has arrived. She is grandchild number seven, and the first granddaughter this side of New Zealand. There does appear to be some possibility that she may enjoy a life of favor. "From orphan to princess," as her father has said, "in a day" – a remarkable transformation.

Once in a while misfortune *can* have good consequences.

Family Facets

Mother Goose and Gander Come to Therapy
(June, 1993)

You have to understand two things. The first is that psychotherapy, which is the work that I do, is by its nature a solitary business. Individuals, couples and families coming to my office expect and deserve privacy, quiet and my full attention, without interruptions or intrusions.

The second thing you have to know is that, although I grew up on a farm, I harbor no romantic illusions about crops, tractors or animals. So you can imagine my consternation when the geese appeared at my office one February afternoon.

My office, which we occupied last November, is on the ground floor of a medical building in West County. Near my office the building is bordered by a small ledge, so the windows, chest high inside the office, are ground-level outside. Beyond the ledge is the building's parking lot.

At first the presence of geese in the parking lot did not seem unusual. Even though there is no water close to the building geese have become commonplace in West County, with its spacious greens and periodic pools, puddles and ponds. When the geese moved up on the ledge outside the window to my office, however, they attracted immediate attention.

Geese are interesting birds. They are social creatures, gathering in groups (called, appropriately, "gaggles"). They mate for life. They tend to return each year to the "family" nest, where the goose and gander work together in reclaiming and refurbishing the nest. And they seldom do anything without conversation, which they do loudly, in raucous squawks and honks.

Although I had noticed the slight depression in the ground on the ledge a foot or so from my window I did not realize what it was until Mother Goose began checking it out, sitting in it momentarily to see if it felt familiar. Although somewhat concerned about the activity on the other side of the window she largely tended to business.

The gander, on the other hand, was very concerned. As seems true of males of many species Gander had little input on the nest itself. His role was as a protector. If Mother sat on the nest he would stand guard, hissing and squawking at anyone passing by. If she elected to sit in the parking lot driveway he would stand defiantly in front of her, stopping all traffic. But he was most determined to drive away the intruders on the other side of the glass.

Although ganders are instinctive protectors of their mates, they are also instinctively cautious. Thus, while Gander wanted to drive me (and my clients) away from his mate's nest, he didn't want to be seen doing it. His tactic was ingenious: he would bang threateningly on the glass with his bill, but he would do so from behind an air-conditioning duct. Since he could not see me, he assumed that I could not see him. A quick review of goose anatomy, however, discloses that while their small heads can hide behind 12 inch ducts their wide bodies cannot. So I could see his body, and hear the banging; and periodically, I would see his head swivel on his long, graceful neck to the side of the duct to see if I was still there.

After a day or two the geese left. But toward the end of March they returned, again with sound and fury. Within a few days Mother Goose was a full-time resident on the nest, this time furbished with leaves, feathers and grass. A few days later we became aware that there were some half-dozen eggs in the nest.

Generally, Mother was quiet on the nest; and as the 30-day nesting period wore on she seemed to hibernate (as, interestingly, the gander did also). But from time to time she displayed considerably interest in what went on in the office. If, as sometimes happens in therapy, voices were raised, she would turn and face into the room. Once, after what I considered a particularly profound observation, I noticed her cock her head to the side, as if in disapproval.

Although she would watch me carefully if I came close to her window she seldom displayed distress except during bad weather or at night. I had always assumed that waterfowl would like water; but geese, at least sitting geese, get rather "testy" in the rain. Nevertheless, we developed a relationship of sorts: she tolerated me; and I grew rather accustomed to her constant presence.

As the days wore on into late April our anticipation, in spite of ourselves, mounted. And so we were rather excited when, on a Wednesday, I noticed cracks and holes in several of the eggs when Mother would stretch her legs. Sure enough, the following day, there were signs of life: at least a half dozen squirming, fuzzy, greenish-yellow babies, looking far too big to have ever squeezed into an egg. They were hard to spot, as Mother tried valiantly to keep them under wing, but a careful observer (which I was) could see heads popping up behind wings or from under her tail. Not surprisingly, my office was a popular place that Thursday.

But time (and as it turns out, a mother goose) marches on: I was out of the office on Friday, but heard that Mother had her flock out on the parking lot Friday morning. By Friday evening they were gone, goose, goslings, gander and all, presumably headed to water. There's been no sight -- nor sound -- of them since.

I hate to admit it, but I rather miss Mother. It seems a bit strange to say that I'm grieving for a goose, but I do find myself approaching the corner near the empty nest cautiously, expecting to see her there. Attachment occurs when you spend time together, it seems, even between man and goose. And, of course, where there is attachment there must inevitably be loss.

I did learn some things, I think, from Mother Goose and Gander, in addition to the relationship between attachment and loss. I learned a bit more about birth and life, at least as it applies to geese. I learned to admire geese, who display many admirable values. I learned to appreciate patience, as exhibited by a goose (and the ever-present gander) sitting for 30 days.

And I learned something about hope: I'll be looking for Mother when she returns to the nest next year. It will be good to see her again.

(Mother did return the following year, and the year after that. We developed a comfortable relationship limited, of course, to only two months each year. But then Mother's comfort level was irretrievably breached.

It was about 7:00 PM, and already dark. A mother and daughter, struggling to repair a severely alienated relationship, were in my office. The daughter, aggrieved by something her mother said, began to wail loudly.

Her shrieks surprised us all, and especially Mother Goose, who rose vertically from her nest. Unfortunately, she had been facing the building and her frightened flight carried her smashing into my window.

The next morning Mother built a new nest a few feet down the ledge in a more secluded (and presumably quieter) spot. In the process she abandoned three eggs outside my window.

I miss Mother each nesting season. But even in moving away she continued to teach me about loss.)

Serena Rose
(November, 1993)

In the end, as the pieces began to come together after all those years, it seemed to be too much, too fast. After a lifetime of not knowing, a decade of wondering, three years of searching, suddenly everything began to come into focus.

It had begun for the man a dozen years earlier with a growing desire to find -- to know -- his birth father, divorced from his mother when the man was only two. There had been no contact, even then, for nearly 40 years. He knew only that his father had remarried, had a child, and had moved to San Francisco.

His only legacy was a few vague recollections, a few unfavorable stories, a few tersely labeled pictures: "Daddy Irv" (a man dressed in 1940s clothing); "Daddy Irv and Serena Rose" (the same man and a baby); "Serena Rose" (the same baby, a few months old, looking unhappy).

Sporadic efforts to find an address or telephone number proved fruitless until the man came upon a "how-to" search manual written by a private investigator. In short order he learned that his father had died in San Francisco in 1980; that he had been a widower for 13 years; that he had been a locksmith for 30 years; and that he lived with his (apparently unmarried) daughter Serena at the time of his death. But at that point the doors again closed: the man could find no information on Serena Rose.

And so it came to be that the man, on his way to Los Angeles for a conference, flew first to San Francisco. He had little to go on: only an address from some three years earlier, found by a data-base search service. He was conscious of considerable ambivalence: the side-trip was expensive, and in all probability would find nothing; but finding anything, as unlikely as that was, was even more frightening.

On the flight to San Francisco the man became violently ill. The flu? More likely, stress.

It turned out to be surprisingly easy. He rented a car at the San Francisco airport and had his first answer within an hour. Finding the three-year-old address he met an elderly (and somewhat intoxicated) man who told him that Serena had previously lived there. He did not have a current address, but suggested that the man call "the Golden Gate Regency." Driving to find a pay phone the man knew what he would learn, realized that he had suspected this all along.

The social worker at the Golden Gate Regional Center confirmed that Serena, mentally retarded, lived in one of their group homes. She was reluctant to provide an address, a reluctance the man shared, until they could be sure Serena could understand what was happening, who he was. But there was an Aunt who lived in San Mateo. The social worker would contact her, give her the man's telephone number.

An hour later, sitting at a window table at Neptune's Palace at the end of Pier 39, the man watched hundreds of sea lions sunning on wooden floats. To his left he could see the hills of San Francisco; to his right, Alcatraz Island.

Over scallops he sorted through questions. They had been here, in San Francisco, all the time. Why had he not looked earlier? In the end, they had been alone together, his father and his sister. What was it like for her when he suddenly died? What was life like for him? Was he imprisoned by his disabled daughter? Would it have helped him if he had known his other child had a Ph.D.? The questions, juxtaposed against the scene of sea lions gathered in small family-like groupings, was overpowering.

The next day, on the way to the airport, he found the cemetery. Wandering among the graves he looked for Block 201, Row B, Number 21. It was marked with a flat gravestone. He saw small pebbles on nearby graves, which he knew meant there had been visitors, that the deceased was not forgotten. Before he left he found a small stone for his father's grave. He may not have known his father, but he was not forgotten.

A week later, after returning home, the man received a call from Serena's Aunt Betty in San Mateo. Betty was stunned by the news of the man's existence: neither her sister nor her brother-in-law had ever mentioned a previous marriage, another child. She was gracious, caring. Widowed herself, she visited Serena each week. She was not sure if Serena would understand, but she would try to tell her she had a brother.

The man was not sure, but he thought that Betty was glad to find out about him herself, also glad to find more family. Betty also told him about Thelma, in whose childhood home his orphaned father had been raised. Thelma lived near Los Angeles, and could, perhaps, provide more answers.

Suddenly everything was coming together: a whole new family vista, a whole new sense of self opening up. It *was* too much, too soon, yes; but it was what he had always wanted, what he had always needed.

He was – finally – finding family.

Personal Lessons

Discovering Self

Three qualities have been part of who I am since I was launched from childhood: a sense of not being safe; feelings of inadequacy; and a profound fear of being unimportant.

This is not to say that I *understood* these aspects of my psyche, or could have articulated them if asked; but to a greater or lesser extent I have always known that they were a part of me, that they *defined* me in a very real sense. I certainly knew that I was fearful; as a child I had even thought of myself as "yellow." Except for things academic I always felt inadequate, less capable -- in things mechanical, athletic, or worldly -- than others around me. And, accordingly, I *presumed* that I was not worthy of others' value. Who, after all, could value a useless coward?

I have not come swiftly to an understanding of these limitations, but I have spent my life trying to overcome them. Most of the things I have done -- both worthy and disappointing -- have, on reflection, been attempts to meet one of these three corresponding needs: for safety, competence, or love.

If I left home to study science in college, it was because I wanted others to see me as smart; and if I ultimately completed a Ph.D., it was to prove that I was competent. If I switched from studying science to pursuing a degree in religion, to enter ministry, it was to find value. If I built an early career in criminal justice, in corrections, it was to confront my own fears, to try to prove -- to myself, if not to others -- that I was not too afraid. And if I looked for love too avidly, never recognizing when it was already at hand, can the reasons be anything but clear?

I remember an evening, as a junior or senior in high school, when I was cruising around town with friends. I recall sitting crammed into the back seat of a classmate's car. I remember someone putting salt into my cherry coke when we stopped at a drive-in. I even recall some of what we thought was witty banter. I remember this so clearly because, to the best of my recollection, it was the only "cruising" I ever did, one of the very few times I was ever with peers outside of class.

When I say I grew up isolated, I mean *isolated*, an only child in an alienated farm family. So I suppose it's not surprising that I've come rather late to this business of "self-awareness."

I was nearly thirty before I began to study psychology, and forty-five before seriously considering doing psychotherapy, but it was these steps that allowed me to begin to pull together disparate pieces, to begin to get to know myself. Better late than never, certainly.

If developmental psychologists are correct a child growing up alone in a disconnected family, with limited contact with peer groups, is likely to have difficulty developing a sense of individuality. "Self-knowledge," in other words, must be built upon a solid family foundation, from which individuality can be developed through transitional relationships with peers.

As has been previously discussed ("Discovering Family," pp. 4-5), my family foundation was shaky at best.

My purpose here is not to cast blame. My parents, overwhelmed and distracted, did the best they could with what they had. But if I am to know myself, to understand how and why I have come to be whom and what I am, I must be honest, or at least as honest as possible at this moment. I am, after all, a product of my fears and doubts.

Still, if I peek objectively at all that has been wrought in my name, it is not so bad. One might, if one could be permitted, feel a bit of pride. I have built, or perhaps stumbled upon and held on to, a large and loving family. I have acquired -- "earned" is probably a more honest term -- impressive credentials. I have performed well in many areas, from welfare worker to corrections specialist to university teacher to psychotherapist. In each of these endeavors I have gained a measure of respect from my peers.

I've even been told that I'm a pretty good writer.

Amazing, isn't it? In the immortal words of Fats Waller, "One never knows, do one?"

Foundations

The Warp
(June, 1991)

I have encountered a curious anomaly. I have discovered what, for lack of a better term, I am calling a "space-time warp." Its exact location is unclear, but it is in southwestern Missouri, somewhere between Springfield and Golden City, where my parents live. I know it is there because I encounter it each time I go home for a visit.

"What happened, Mr. Spock? And where in the universe are we?"

"Uncertain, Captain. Sensors report we are several million light-years away from where we were two minutes ago. It appears we have encountered a wrinkle in the space-time fabric; perhaps we are in a parallel universe."

My trip through the warp manifests itself in many ways. First, everything looks different on the other side, as if I have been abruptly transported to a time long past. Surroundings appear barren, buildings ancient, even cars and people conforming to looks of an earlier, agrarian America.

In addition, people seem different. Like a Twilight Zone episode, they seem to move more slowly, marching to slightly different music, with focus and concerns alien to those I have come to know and value.

Then, finally, *I* am different on the other side. I feel younger – too young, at times, even childlike. In fact, it is almost as if I become younger the further I travel into the warp (or at least until I reach my parents, at which point I remain about 13). This is typically not a pleasant sensation, being accompanied by a sense of becoming uncertain, helpless, and feeling out of control. It is as if *I* have become the alien.

This condition seems to last as long as I am on the far side of the warp. Others, such as my wife, are not affected (although there is some evidence a differing space-time warp may exist for her somewhere between St. Louis and Boston). Remarkably, I have always been able to find the exact spot to re-enter the rift and return to my real self in St. Louis time and space.

But each time I wonder if I will be able to make it all the way back.

"Captain, my calculations indicate that we have only 12 nano-seconds before the space-time rift closes forever. We have to return while we can."

"Thank you, Mr. Spock. Mr. Sulu, warp factor nine. Let's hit that rift while we can!"

$\mathcal{er}$

Is there a moral here? "A rift in time saves nine?" Or, "Where there's a rift, there's a way?" Perhaps, of course, this is only a "mind-warp!"

I do suspect, however, that this phenomenon is not unique to me (although the geographical locations of others' rifts will vary). It is, of course, my business as a psychologist to help others learn to navigate their space-time warps. But navigators can get lost too, can't they?

Going Home Alone
(April, 1992)

I flew to Springfield, Missouri, with actor John Goodman recently. I was on my way to visit my parents in Golden City. Goodman was in Springfield to finally join the fraternity he pledged, but could not join because he was too poor, while a student at Southwest Missouri State.

My compulsion for honesty requires me to tell you that I did not know Goodman was on the flight, even though it was a *very* small airplane. I only glimpsed him, across the terminal, after the rental car agent mentioned the "celebrity" on the flight. It turns out that being a public radio talk-show host in St. Louis does not qualify one for "celebrity" status.

I do not know how Goodman's stay in Springfield went. My visit to Golden City went well, considering.. .

Considering that I went home alone.

I have always found it difficult to remain an adult in the presence of my parents. (This must be a somewhat familiar experience, for I get understanding murmurs when I ask groups how long they have to be home before they "feel like a child.") Perhaps my response is because my mother still refers to me as "Ronnie." Perhaps it is because they both seem to persist in seeing me as a child: bright, well intentioned, but too young to really understand.

Most likely, though, the problem – certainly, the part I can do something about – lies with me. I am quite sure that the first step toward improvement requires that I take ownership of my juvenile feelings. If I feel fourteen, it must be – according to my cognitive theory textbook – because in my parents' home I encounter cues that connect with events from childhood, physical or behavioral reminders that "hook" into fourteen-year-old feeling states. Or –according to my family systems textbooks – because the interactive patterns, reflecting unresolved issues between us, continue to repeat patterns laid down in childhood.

Whatever the cause, the effect is often uncomfortable (probably for us all). My solution, in recent years, has been to resort to a time-honored male ploy: let my wife handle it. Thus, we usually make these visits together. Because she is not afflicted with the same memories and cues I am, she can continue to listen and chatter even as I become emotionally distressed and silent.

(Actually, anyone knowing my Marilyn knows that "chatter" is not in her repertoire; but then anyone knowing my mother knows that it does not matter, because all one can do is listen, anyway.) Furthermore, if the situation gets bad enough – if I appear in danger of permanent withdrawal – Marilyn will suggest a walk, where she and I can "process" me back into a semblance of sociability.

But Marilyn was making a trip to Boston, to deal with her own memories; so it seemed a good time for both of us to make separate visits. So, alone – except, of course, for John Goodman – I visited Golden City.

As I said, things went well, considering. Since I have been able to identify a few of the comments and phrases that precipitate my juvenile regressive psychoses I was able to respond better. And, as previously observed, the primary useful social skill involved *is*, after all, listening.

So it was a pretty good trip. I was able to spend some time with my father, who is not doing well. I was able to listen to my mother. And I didn't really feel fourteen.

I'd say it was more like seventeen.

On the other hand, John Goodman never knew I was on the plane either.

Schindlerjuden
(March, 1994)

Wartime, like all human craziness, produces strange heroes. Witness Oskar Schindler, who could only succeed by becoming rich on the losses of others, but who saved a generation of souls in the process.

Reb Mendel Stavisker left Pultusk, near Warsaw, Poland for the United States in 1903 to join three brothers in Utica, New York. Upon arriving he took the "new" family name and became Max Stone. His two oldest sons, Samuel (14) and David (12), joined him within a year; his wife Liba Pia (Elizabeth) came a year later.

Max assumed his trade as a baker; he later moved to Detroit, Michigan. Sam Stone, a motion-picture operator, married Sylvia Hocheiser, of Hungarian descent, in 1918. They had four children. The eldest, Gertrude, married Irving Schwartz, an orphan youth of German descent, in 1937. The marriage lasted less than three years. One son was born, named Ronald.

When Oskar Schindler turned up in Krakow, Poland in the late 1930s Europe was plunging toward war. Anti-Semitism was rife, with Jews denied property and herded into ghettos. Schindler was unknown, but he soon ingratiated himself to the German military hierarchy.

Coming to Poland with little or nothing he convinced a Jew named Itshak Stern to help him "buy" a bankrupt kitchenware factory with Jewish money to sell pots and pans to the German army. "Hiring" Jewish labor as virtual slaves, Schindler paid "wages" (and bribes) to German army officers. He retained the plant's Jewish manager to run the plant. Schindler's skill was in marketing, wining and dining the German military leadership.

Schindler was immediately successful. While Poland disintegrated, and while Jews were being shipped to slaughter by the millions, Schindler's factory, run by *Schindlerjuden* (Schindler's Jews), churned out pots and pans (and money). When the order came to remove all Jews from Krakow Schindler created his own prison "sub-camp," co-opting a disturbed prison camp commander named Amon Goethe.

In the midst of snowfalls of ash from burned Jewish bodies, while German officers arbitrarily murdered prisoners, Schindler protected "his" Jews. When the "final solution" was imposed and all Jews were directed to Auswitch Schindler used his profits to "buy" more than 1100 of his workers and their families, transporting them to his native Czechoslovakia to establish a German munitions plant. The legend is that the plant never produced a working artillery shell.

At the end of the war Schindler's Jews were "liberated" by a lone Soviet Army officer. Their plight was epitomized in their homelessness: they could not return to Poland, and they dared not go west. But they were alive. Schindler, as a Nazi munitions manufacturer, fled west, into a life of failed businesses and a failed marriage.

I have always understood that it was an accident of geography that resulted in my being born in 1938 in Detroit, Michigan, rather than in Poland. As a result the holocaust has always taken on a fearful fascination, a personal horror.

Steven Spielberg's monumental film of Oskar Schindler's story was adapted from a powerful 1982 book by Thomas Keneally. I watched "Schindler's List" from a great distance, as if through a tunnel. It was as close as I could allow myself to come.

"Schindler's List" is expected to be a big winner at this year's Academy Awards. Done largely in black and white, in a "documentary" style, it is at once horrifying and compelling. I do not know if it is a "great" film, or if the directing or acting was good. I only know it was overwhelming to watch.

There is a sense in which the overwhelming horror of "Schindler's List" becomes too much, numbing. In contrast, for example, the single searing incident of horror that pierced Meryl Streep's "Sophie's Choice" could not be avoided, encapsulating the terror of the holocaust into a single scene.

But numbing or not, horrifying or not, Spielberg has created a necessary testimony to man's capacity for evil – and to man's capacity for heroism as well. "Schindler's List" should be seen by every person old enough to grasp its meaning and tolerate its pain.

We must never forget.

Farm Field Fantasy
(October, 1994)

In his wonderful *Shoeless Joe*, from which the movie, "Field of Dreams," was made, William Kinsella suggested that one need only "build it" – a baseball diamond – and the players, past or present, "will come."

It may be so in fiction, or on the sandlot, and perhaps even in the minors; but it is no longer so in "the show" (which is, as we learned from "Bull Durham," what baseball players call the major leagues). Finally, mercifully, after several comatose weeks without meaningful negotiations to end a labor dispute the major league baseball season was declared dead.

Here lies Baseball 1994. RIP.

It was not always so. As a boy, an only child on an isolated farm in Missouri, baseball was a lifeline, a connection to the larger world. I spent hours listening to games, and even more hours dreaming about them later. In fantasies *I* was Country Slaughter, rounding second and heading for third; or Marty Marion, diving for the ball deep in the hole and bounding up to catch the batter by a whisker at first.

My father once "complained" (teasingly, I later realized) to my mother that I was a hazard on the tractor because "by the time Slaughter gets to third he's plowed up half a row of corn." I was embarrassed, wondering how he knew.

My "mentor" in the metaphors of baseball was Harry Caray, the then youthful broadcaster who was more fan than factual, who could make a game he created off Western Union wires more exciting than it could ever be in person. For me, the St. Louis Cardinals *were* Harry Caray, so much so that it was his autograph I sought on one of my annual expeditions to St. Louis to see a game.

And wonderful metaphors for life they are, the metaphors of baseball, such as

- *It's not over until the last man is out* (*i.e.,* hope);
- *You've got to "play within yourself"* (*i.e.,* accept limits);
- *It's only a game* (*i.e.,* perspective); but
- *Always hustle* (*i.e.,* seek excellence).

And it is in baseball that one learns that the very best hitters hit safely only one-third of the time, demonstrating forcefully that *perfection* is unattainable, is *not* the same thing as excellence.

As a youth, circumstances prevented my "playing out" childhood fantasies. My opportunity to act out the dream came years later, as an already paunchy adult, when I joined a slo-pitch church softball team. I was not, in truth, a very good player: I had little batting power, no running speed, and a weak throwing arm. But I discovered that I *could* throw lobbed strikes (a slo-pitch requirement), and suddenly I found myself the starting pitcher on the church's "B" team.

It was a dream come true. I even pitched to E. J. Junior, the football Cardinal's linebacker who was "keeping in shape" while on suspension. (He hit a massive home run). My "ultimate" game was the one in which I was pitching a shut-out entering the seventh and final inning, and in which I had "powered" a triple over the drawn in left fielder's head.

But like all dreams, I awoke too soon. The manager, concerned that I could not "hold" our one-run lead, took me out and inserted himself to pitch the final inning. He lost the game.

Given the money that is made from baseball today I am sure that the players deserve the millions they make; but they do not play the game that you and I played as kids (or slo-pitch adults). I remember a friend, while a student at Rolla, that had once won six straight games for the Houston Colts, then a Cardinal's Texas League farm team. He had left the team because of his father's death, and had never returned. I offered to "catch" him in some nostalgic warming-up: I never touched his curve ball, and his half- speed fast balls left my hand swollen for days.

What is at stake in the major league strike is money, where the issue is the business of baseball. This action is no more about baseball than is multi-national corporate raiding about being an entrepreneur. Who cares if the millionaire players or billionaire owners win? A pox on both their houses!

If the strike-end of the season kills the dream, so be it; perhaps it's time to grow up, to give up childhood dreams. But, having done so, we may come to understand that the dream, as William Kinsella has tried to tell us, was not about childhood, not even about baseball.

The dream, my friends, is about life, your life and mine. In spite of the strike, the farm-field fantasy still lives.

Amos Hart and the Search for Self
(May, 1998)

We went to *Chicago* recently, and I found myself. Or, at least, a piece of myself.

But not in the city. Rather, I "found myself" at the Fox Theater production of the smash Broadway revival of a 1970s Bob Fosse musical.

As restaged by Ann Reinking, who played Roxy Hart in the original production and again in the recent revival, *Chicago* is an unrelentingly cynical look at 20th Century America set, mostly, in the women's section of the Cook County Jail in the late 1920s. Introduced as "a story of murder, greed, corruption, violence, exploitation, adultery, and treachery -- all those things we all hold near and dear to our hearts," *Chicago* is raunchy, bawdy, and thoroughly delightful.

I must confess that my love affair with *Chicago* is not as recent as these comments suggest. I first saw the musical in a local production a few years ago, and the CD of the Ann Reinking –Bebe Neuwirth Broadway revival is a regular on my personal play-list. But juxtaposed with recent self-explorations, enjoying it again helped crystallize insight.

The story revolves around Roxy Hart, a Chicago chorus girl married to a remarkably unassuming mechanic. Frustrated and bored in her marriage, Roxy takes up with Fred Casely, a night club regular, then shoots him when he tries to dump her. In jail Roxy discovers a new world of murderous women (including Velma Kelly, who murdered her sister and husband when she discovered them doing the "spread-eagle" together), a tough matron (Mama Morton, who runs her brood according to the principle of "reciprocity:" Mama can get you anything for a few bucks) and a slick, silver-tongued lawyer (Billy Flynn, who had a gift for getting girls off with "razzle-dazzle").

But perhaps the most fascinating character is Amos, Roxy's poor cuckolded husband. Amos seems always a step or two behind, used by everybody and never quite "getting it," stumbling along as the only decent person in the story. He is, by his own observation, invisible.

Amos sums up his life in a song-and-dance lament filled with humor and pathos:

"Cellophane / Mister Cellophane / Shoulda been my name / Mister Cellophane / Cause you can look right through me / Walk right by me / and never know I'm there."

I found something of myself in Amos' lament, and I suspect that I am not alone. I understand being invisible, always seeming to be a step late. As a metaphor for life "Mister Cellophane" works as well for me as it does for Amos Hart. Like Amos, I've struggled most of my life to be noticed. Most of my successes and many of my significant failures have been tied up in seeking recognition.

I left the farm at seventeen, becoming the first in my family to attend college, as much for escape as for any other reason. But I did not want just *any* college. I applied only to science and engineering schools, including the top-rated schools in the country: M.I.T., Cal Tech, Carnegie, the University of Chicago. Since I had no money, going to any of these schools was not possible; but I derived a great deal of satisfaction at just being *accepted* at M.I.T. and Chicago.

In the end I enrolled at the state technical school, The Missouri School of Mines and Engineering (and even this was only possible because of low in-state fees and a scholarship). But even there I majored in physics, not the more practical engineering. It was, I now see, all about *recognition,* being *seen* as bright enough.

After two years I ran out of steam (and ran into Advanced Calculus, Heat and Thermodynamics, and Atomic Physics) and transferred to Baylor University, having reengineered myself in a more suitable direction.

This need to be seen (or see myself) as *competent* has always been with me, as much a part of my reality as the ever-present conviction of inadequacy it combats. Given the circumstances, enrollment in a Ph.D. program (of some type) was inevitable: school was always the one thing I knew I could do well.

I suspect Amos Hart's "cellophane" helps to explain another constant of my life: volunteering. I've taught Sunday School classes, served on church committees and boards, and preached dozens of "volunteer" sermons, always gravitating to leadership roles in every church I've attended. I was president of the local "Volunteers in Probation and Parole" board for ten years, and served more than ten years as editor of the local psychological association's newsletter, *after* previously being treasurer and president.

Why? For a kid who always fell between the cracks, feeling unnoticed and unrespected, I suspect that it's always been more about *recognition* than service.

That's all right, I suppose. I have come to understand that the desire for recognition is not inherently negative. Rather, like any need, it is most likely to be dangerous when it operates unacknowledged, in the dark.

But, of course, that's where Mister Cellophane would think he is operating, isn't it?

The Baker Effect
(October 2002)

I played God once, in an off-campus dramatic production while I was a student at Baylor University in Waco, Texas. It was not an easy role.

I was reminded of this a few months ago when the Baylor alumni magazine, *The Baylor Line*, featured a story about Paul Baker. Baker was the director of the unlikely Baylor Studio Theater from 1941 until 1963, during which time he impacted hundreds of students. "Unlikely," because the Southern Baptist's flagship university was an unlikely host for an innovative experimental dramatics program that attracted attention by the likes of Charles Laughton and Burgess Meredith.

"Innovative," as demonstrated by a studio theater featuring six stages surrounding the audience, who sat on swivel chairs so they could follow the action; or by a 1953 production of *Othello* featuring three Othellos and three Iagos, reflecting differing psychological aspects of the characters; or, most famously, a 1956 production of *Hamlet*, with Meredith in the title role, again splitting the main character into three parts, with actors representing each part shadowing Meredith's Hamlet and echoing his words.

Baker's fame was such that he was able to persuade Eugene O'Neill's widow to allow Baylor to produce *A Long Day's Journey into Night* in 1962. Mrs. O'Neill had allowed the production on one condition: that not one word be altered. Unfortunately, the production was closed by Baylor President Abner McCall after complaints by leaders of a Baptist youth group that had seen the profanity-laced production. A year later Baker and his entire drama faculty resigned and relocated at Trinity University in San Antonio.

I never met Baker, although I was a student at Baylor in 1958 and 1959; but I was affected by him in that curious way that one person's "effect" may ricochet from individual to individual. While at Baylor, I fell in with a group that included one of Baker's graduate students. When that student began casting a play he had written that featured Satan and God as "sideline commentators" for a drama based on the life of the Apostle Paul, I was cast as God (apparently because I had "a big voice").

The student cast as Satan and I were to observe and comment on the action from railings on either side of the stage (actually a church's altar area), with text loosely adapted from the Book of Job. I remember well the director's attempt to implement Baker's "philosophy," involving integration of the "senses" into performance. "Move like a cat," he instructed Satan. He ordered me to "move like a mountain." I envied Satan.

In the end, after demonstrating that I was not nearly creative enough to figure out how a mountain might move, I was instructed to stand absolutely still -- no mean feat for a 45 minute production. Meanwhile, Satan got to twist and prance around, in moves I could never have made even if I had gotten that part.

The production was, as clearly as I can recall, a success. My clearest memory was the irony that someone so certain of his own incompetence could actually portray God. Perhaps, thinking back on it, that was the genius of Paul Baker's philosophy at work.

I commented earlier about a "ricochet effect." A few years after leaving Baylor, while volunteering with a youth group in a Baptist Church in Norwalk, California, I directed a group of students in a blatantly derivative play I had written about the Apostle Paul.

Understand, please, that I had absolutely nothing to draw on, in leading these teen-agers, except my experience in that one play. Naturally, the production lurched toward play-date with all the predictable problems: lines not learned, kids not showing up for practice, others upset with their roles or someone else's performances, and everyone angry at me.

You will appreciate, then, the impact as everything came together for the performance and a dozen or so students experienced themselves being part of a creative enterprise. I still recall being hugged enthusiastically by several teen-aged girls -- something I never experienced before or afterwards -- as the lights fell at the end of the performance.

From Paul Baker to his students, to other students who never crossed his path, to still other students a thousand miles away and only encountering glimpses of his thinking: such can be the effect of a single individual. One can never know where (or how often) a thoughtful observation or encouraging word will land.

Relationships

Remembering Circles
(February, 1994)

I arrived in Waco, Texas in January, 1958, to attend Baylor University. Naive, starry-eyed, fresh off the farm (by way of two years at the Rolla School of Mines), my plan was to be a Baptist preacher.

Fortunately, not only for me but for the Baptist Church, there have been many turns in the road since Baylor. But Waco was a significant stop along my life's twisting trail. I learned a lot about myself there. I found that I could "make it" on my own. I even met and married my first wife in Waco.

And it was at Baylor that I met Dr. George Humphrey.

George Humphrey was a Baptist minister, a professor of Religion at Baylor University, and, at that time, the Chairperson of the Religion Department. Although he could have obtained pastorates in large, important churches, he considered his teaching role more important. "In a church," he would say, "I would speak to a few hundred; but in teaching I can impact hundreds who, themselves, will impact hundreds."

Since I arrived at Baylor already classified as a senior I soon found myself in one of George Humphrey's courses. Not surprisingly, considering the 35 years that have elapsed, I do not remember what he taught; but I do vividly remember him.

George Humphrey had a reputation as a healer. He regularly served interim pastorates in troubled Baptist churches in the Waco area, healing the scars of conflicts and splits. He defined his life by a favorite poem, one that he repeated in every class:

He drew a circle that shut me out,
Heretic, rebel, a will to flout;
But love and I had the wit to win:
We drew a circle that took him in.

The day came when a final examination in one of Dr. Humphrey's classes intersected with a personal state of angst produced, as I recall, by the loss of a girlfriend. Although normally a good student, I found myself agitated and unable to concentrate.

I left the classroom in tears and, not knowing what else to do, went to Dr. Humphrey's office. (George Humphrey always administered his tests on the honor system.) Disregarding my sense of failure, he gently and unobtrusively acknowledged my pain. Neither preaching nor moralizing, he simply suggested that I come back the next day and retake the test. That is, he "drew a circle that took me in."

My understanding is that our particular conception of "eternal life" is peculiarly western, a Hellenization of ancient Egyptian, Persian and Semitic beliefs. Yet it is also a direct consequence, I suspect, of the development of consciousness: once I can think of myself as an object I find it difficult to conceive of my "self" as no longer existing. Whether one's sense of eternity is perceived as a heaven and hell, or in terms of reincarnation, or in some pantheistic formula is a function of one's faith, of the mythology into which one is born or which one acquires. In an objective sense, in the way we *know* what we know, we can never be sure about eternity.

But the desire to *continue to be* seems universal. Perhaps one way we can recognize continuation may be through the things that remain after us. Some of these are material, of course; but ultimately the most eternal are less tangible: ideas, connections, memories. And ultimately, I suspect, it is in memories that we most assuredly remain.

In preparing this reflection on George Humphrey I called the current chairperson of the Department of Religion at Baylor University. I did not realize that George Humphrey had been born in Missouri, although he had spent his entire adult life in Texas.

I also learned that he had died a few years earlier. There was sadness, of course, at this news. But joy remained. George Humphrey is still alive for me.

It is in memories that we find eternity.

Encountering Old Friends
(July, 1994)

The gray-haired man walked up to me at the airport as I was trying to find a white courtesy telephone. I was somewhat distracted, trying to get a room unlocked for my "fear of flying" group. We were already late, there was a pilot coming to talk with the group, and there were several anxious group members, so I did not want interruptions. "Are you Ron Scott?" the man asked. Warily, I confessed. "I'm Jim Pugh," he said.

I looked at the man for the first time. Jim Pugh had been a close high school friend and my first college roommate. Although we exchanged holiday card and letters each year, we had not seen each other for over 30 years. "Of course you are," I said, as if I would have recognized him if he had not seen me first.

Fortunately, the concourse agent (with the key) and the pilot arrived at the same time, and I was able to leave the anxious group in the comforting hands of an ever-confident TWA First Officer. As a result Jim and I and his wife, Sandie, whom I had never met, were able to talk for a few minutes. They were on their way home to Seattle, where they both build airplanes for Boeing, from the Bahamas.

Jim Pugh was a good kid back in Mt. Vernon, Missouri, in the early 1950s. He was well liked, a class leader, on all the sports teams, as was common in small schools. One friend described Jim as "big enough to hunt bears with a switch," so it was not surprising that he played basketball and was a lineman in football.

I always considered our friendship surprising, but then I considered it strange that anyone would like me at that time. Looking back on it, our relationship was probably not so surprising at all: we shared interests, and we probably admired each other.

I know I admired Jim. He was all the things I thought I should be but knew I could never be. He lived "in town;" I lived miles out, in "the country." He played sports; I could not. He dated girls (not just girls, but the Principal's daughter!); girls scared the bejeebers out of me. The only thing I had going for me, I thought, was my "brains," a somewhat dubious distinction that would only have branded me a nerd if the term had existed in those dark ages.

And even that quality was called into question our first year at the Rolla School of Mines when I struggled to cope with college, classes and life off the farm while Jim showed the way. Each evening, as I wandered the dorm halls avoiding chemistry, analytic geometry and other studies, Jim would sit stolidly at his desk, hour after hour, working steadily. Never having had to learn how to study, lacking the organizational skills and discipline needed, I expressed my envy with disdain and sarcasm.

At the end of the year we went separate ways. Jim remained in the dorm. I fled to a room in a private home, needing to strike out on my own, to master (or at least begin to confront) life alone. Eventually I left Rolla, transferring to Baylor University, beginning the quest for self and service that would eventually lead to psychotherapy. Jim stayed, graduated, and became the engineer he was destined to be.

But we, or at least I, remained connected, at least in spirit. When I wrote him that I was engaged I was disappointed to learn that he was already married. We both divorced, and even remarried on about the same schedule. Although I wandered from career to career Jim continued at Boeing, designing environmental systems. Our contact was limited to annual holiday cards.

He remained, always, the man I wished I was, more symbol than fact. That symbolism was demonstrated when he recognized me in the airport, despite 30 years and more pounds, under gray hair and behind a gray beard, when I knew I would never have recognized him without the reminder of a name and context

But the contact, brief as it was, brought reality to symbolism. Jim has also aged, with lines in his face. Meeting his second wife (a delightful lady who seemed genuinely interested in meeting this person previously known only as a name) said clearly that he also has known the pain of divorce, loneliness, and the stresses of a blended family. The realities of our own experiences make it possible to flesh out the realities of others' lives.

We exchanged cards, agreeing to write, expecting to see each other at the upcoming (40th!) high school reunion next year. I mentioned our interest in visiting the Northwest, and Jim encouraged us to include them in any plans. Despite the brevity, despite the 30 years, there was still a sense of closeness, of valuing and being valued.

It was good to see Jim. I'm glad he recognized me. I recognized more of me, too, in the process.

Finding the Extraordinary in Ordinary Places
(October, 1995)

The narrow strip of trees that follows the stream behind our house appears rich and verdant in midsummer, with varying shapes and shades of green, populated by a surprising variety of roaming and flying wildlife. Against the growing light of a recent dawn, amid the morning calls of resident birds, one tree, which has not leafed this year, stood out. Still tall and straight, it displayed a scattering of nests, testimony of years of service. Along its branches were knots, evidence of prior events in the life of the tree. Birds hopped from branch to branch, stark against the lightening sky, risking being seen to gain a better view. Within an ordinary scene the lone bare tree seemed extraordinary.

I sat that morning, gazing at the panorama of the ever-changing constancy of life before me, and thought about my good friend Mel Rubenstein, who died August 11th.

Mel Rubenstein had been a psychiatrist and consultant in St. Louis for nearly half a century. Arriving from the Menninger Foundation in 1949, he had been in private practice, was an emeritus staff member of Jewish Hospital, and had been a psychiatric consultant for Edgewood Children's Center for 40 years, and also consulted for the General Protestant Children's Home and the Annie Malone Children's Home.

Mel was a member of a vanishing breed: psychiatrists who practiced psychotherapy. Trained analytically, he gradually abandoned these roots and adopted a much more eclectic style. Years ago, with an office on Olive in the Central West End, he was affectionately known as "the Gaslight Shrink." In later years he developed a joint psychotherapy practice with his wife, sociologist Dr. Jayne Burks, with whom he had written a well-received book on "temperament type."

Raised in Chicago, the son of a grocer, Mel learned to love baseball at the feet of his immigrant mother, who knew suffering as a lifelong Cubs fan. Although he had been active in the St. Louis' Jewish community he later, with his wife Jayne, joined a small Presbyterian Church in St. Louis County. As far as I know Mel is still the only person who has been designated an "elder" in a Presbyterian church without renouncing his Jewish faith.

I met Mel Rubenstein in 1984 when I began visiting that church. Facing personal difficulties and in the midst of a major career change, from the University that had not granted me tenure to private practice. I was immediately attracted to him. First, he was a psychotherapist, *doing* what I wanted to do. Second, he was Jewish, in a Presbyterian Church. (I have always been conscious of my heritage, even though I have never practiced it religiously or culturally.)

In addition, Mel was intellectually curious, a quality I had always embodied, but too often felt I carried alone. Most importantly, he was *accepting* -- in fact it would never occur to him to be otherwise.

Quietly, without either of us realizing or consciously addressing it, Mel became something special to me, a mentor, a model for much of what I was becoming. This is not to suggest that he taught me how to do therapy, for we seldom discussed psychotherapy (although he did tell stories). Neither did he seek to teach me anything about being Jewish, although he often shared his sense of his own Jewishness. Nor did he ever seek to tell me what to believe, or how to live.

Mel Rubenstein mentored a *way of living*, an acceptance, both of himself and of me, that gave meaning and freedom. He could not have known, I suppose, but it was exactly what I needed. I am today a better therapist, a more comfortably spiritual person, and better educated because of him. Most importantly, I believe I am more accepting, especially of myself. Perhaps, in the end, that is what mentoring is all about.

As I gaze at the leafless tree in the morning light threads of understanding weave among the textures of my grief. The roots and branches of its life will continue to provide meaning and support through the years to come. There may be emptiness, but one can never lose the experiences of life.

It is extraordinary what shade a leafless tree can give.

Too Soon Good-bye
(September, 2003)

God, I hate to write this.

When I arrived at my office on August 20th I found a letter from Larry Kogan containing an insurance reimbursement for one of my clients, inexplicably sent to him. There was no note. Brevity of action was always Larry's style. The envelope was postmarked August 18th.

What made the letter difficult to see was not the insurance company's error, but the fact that Larry Kogan had died, suddenly, during a late-afternoon golf game on Monday, August 18th. Apparently, he dropped the envelope in the mail on his way to the course.

I have known Larry Kogan for nearly 20 years, first as an instructor and later as a colleague and friend. I can say without exaggeration that much of who I am today -- both as a psychotherapist and as a man -- I owe to him.

Larry had been, as my wife observed, very possibly my closest friend. Even though we saw each other less frequently in recent years, the easy sense of intimacy, of knowing and being known, remained every time we got together.

But I was certainly not alone in being touched by Larry. As a social activist whose strong feelings about Viet Nam led him into conflict with the justice system; as a co-founder, a few years later, of Left Bank Books; as a teacher and mentor for dozens of area therapists; and as an individual, marital and family therapist for more than twenty-five years his *imprimatur* has been felt throughout the community.

But such "public" aspects of Larry do not begin to define the man himself. His family and close friends knew him to be a man of passions -- for his work and social justice, yes, but even more for his wife and children, for golf, and for cooking. Larry's wife, Deni, has called him "the best cook in town." My experience supports that judgement. In particular, he was known for his desserts.

In our work together on the intricacies and eccentricities of being male in a society that has long denied men full emotional citizenship Larry and I often talked about our experiences as sons, husbands and fathers. He loved Deni and his children; but, even more importantly, he was willing and able to let them know. He was unabashedly proud as his son, Josh, grew into manhood and embarked on a year of study and volunteering in Israel; and as daughter Sarah developed into a beautiful and talented 16-year-old. And he made frequent trips to his roots in Cleveland, Ohio, where his 87-year-old mother, Sylvia Kogan, continues to live.

Larry loved all sports, following the Indians and Browns of his native Cleveland as well as the Cardinals and Rams; played basketball in his youth; and played tennis regularly with friends; but he was, ultimately, a golfer. Already, inevitably, the myth has begun to grow: it is reported that Larry passed out on the first hole last Monday, but got up to finish the hole at par; then, chipping in from off the green he birdied the second hole before again collapsing on the third.

As a new therapist acutely aware of my inadequacies I enrolled, in 1984, in the marriage and family therapy certificate program Larry and Richard Laitman ran at Washington University. I remember thinking of Richard as the more organized instructor, but Larry made more of an emotional impact. Their program provided a way of thinking about and working with problems that I continue to use today.

A few years later, I received a call from Larry asking if I would be interested in being part of a group practice. I was at once astounded and honored: I had no idea that I had impressed someone I had so admired as a potential colleague. During the next few years we worked across the hall from each other. We conducted groups, wrote papers and attended conferences as we explored men's and other issues together.

But truthfully, Larry's greatest gift to me was not in what he taught or what we worked on together. The most important thing he gave to an aging adolescent who never felt good enough or worthy enough was *acceptance* – dare I say love? – that allowed *me* to better accept and love *me*. I wish I could have told him that sometime before he reached that third hole on Monday.

Mary Patton, who moved into the office I left in the Ballas Road suite, mentioned at Larry's funeral that she had gone into his office on the Tuesday after his death. On his desk, she said, was a note he had left himself: "call Ron for lunch."

Larry died much too young, at 59. Yes, I do understand that death is a part of life, and that it comes to all of us. But I don't have to like it.

Coping

Holiday Blues
(December, 1988)

It has always sneaked up on me, that seasonal "holiday depression." As if it didn't happen every year, I have been surprised anew to realize that I was a bit darker than usual, a little more distant, slightly more contained. Only when Marilyn observed that everything seemed to make me angry; or when I found myself more upset than usual at other drivers; or when the frowns and clenched teeth turned into headaches did I realize that it was happening again.

I used to wonder each year why it happened and wish that it would not; but absence of understanding only made it worse. The holiday season demands cheerfulness; being gloomy only adds to the guilt. To protect others from my dark mood I would become silent; and yet, in the very act of protecting, I punished.

Oh, it is not that the season has no trials. It *is* a distracting time. Clients always seem more distraught; and I fear I am less effective with them. There never seems to be enough time. I rush to the store in a spare two hours, but since I never organize my gift-giving I can never decide what to buy. So I buy nothing, but end exhausted, a rare "opportunity" gone. And the radio plays carols incessantly. If "The 12 Days of Christmas" comes on one more time. . . .

There are always too many parties at which I am uncomfortable making small talk with too many people I don't really know, and eating (to nurture my anxieties) far too much. Another trip to the mall, where I buy a gift that I'm not sure I like and I am sure that Marilyn will dislike, but my feet hurt and I'm tired. And "The 12 Days of Christmas" is playing at the mall. . . .

Marilyn always comes to my rescue and goes shopping with me, and even though I feel bad needing her help I need her help. We still can't find everything, because I'm still not organized. We do find a shirt for my father and a potpourri pot box for a colleague, although my feet still hurt, and I am tired, and "The 12 Days of Christmas" . . . .

Last year the cat peed on my father's shirt and on the potpourri pot box. It snowed and turned to ice and my tire went flat and I spent my last free afternoon waiting for the auto club because a gorilla had put the tire on and I could not loosen the lug nuts and I broke one off. So, I didn't finish shopping, but I *did* hear "The 12 Days of Christmas" three times while waiting. . . .

It always seems to sneak up on me, this time of year. I wait – it seems almost in vain – for the gloom to lift and the "spirit" to hit. And then, almost at the last moment, it seems, the gates come down and the inexplicable seems clearer.

What is clearer is that I do not understand and do not need to understand. It does not matter that I have trouble buying gifts and am uncomfortable at parties and have too little time. It does not matter that the weather is bad and that tires go flat and that the same carols keep being played. It does not matter because that is not what the holidays are all about.

The holidays are not about gifts and parties and shopping and cats that pee. The holidays are about *hope*. They are metaphors for love, and reaching out, and sharing. And in those metaphors, somewhere, lies the answer, and I can, if only for a few short hours, regain the holiday spirit.

I'll be glad when that time comes this year. I know it will; it always has. I'm looking forward to it. I only hope the radio is off.

Reflections on a Painful Wednesday
(November, 1990)

On a recent Wednesday, with nothing on my schedule except six clients, several issues to be resolved in the new practice group I am joining, and all the organizing necessary for relocation of offices, my body decided the time was right to launch a kidney stone.

Readers who are members of the "I had a stone" club will immediately empathize; the rest of you should feel fortunate you cannot.

Stones moving from the kidney to the bladder create irritation that produces spasms, which are the source of the pain. The pain has been variously described as a "hot poker in the side;" a "corkscrew;" and "comparable to labor." I cannot comment on the third description, but the first two seem accurate enough.

Emergency room personnel tend to be cavalier about pain, at least until they are sure what the problem is (or, more precisely, what it is not). So one must endure hours of questions, blood tests, and X-rays (from every conceivable position, including ones one could not achieve in a pain-free state) before obtaining even slight chemical relief. Once you know what the problem is you know you will survive. But with this kind of pain you're not sure you want to.

Afterward, recuperating during an overnight observation at St. Luke's (both in and after a Demerol induced fog), I had time to reflect:

First, self-hypnosis is not very useful with kidney stones. On the other hand moaning, although a clear violation of the "macho" code, does help a little. Second, X-ray tables are uniformly uncomfortable, in part because they all seem to have built-in refrigeration systems. Third, Demerol does not really relieve pain, but it provides such a "buzz" that you don't care. Furthermore, you don't care what they give you: you quickly decide you will deal with any after-effects, like addiction, after the pain is gone.

Pain is, I think, a great "leveler." It is no respecter of class, income or intelligence (although the wealthy and/or insured will certainly have more access to medical treatment and thus to relief). It is also one experience almost everyone has had, so it provides a common ground upon which we can all walk. Pain can be all-consuming during the time it exists, but after it has passed (no pun intended) it is, fortunately, sometimes hard to remember.

It did help, during my five-hour ordeal, to remind myself that there would be an "afterwards." And life does go on. Clients await, or are rescheduled; groups organize; and relocation planning resumes. When we arrived home Thursday morning we passed several police cars. Helicopters hovered overhead, and even Channel 5 was on hand. It seems the last of four escapees from the Medium Security Prison had been sighted in the woods behind us.

It is good to know that there is more to life than pain.

Riverfront Confession
(September, 1994)

It was one of those disturbing events that mar an otherwise delightful day. Our daughter Stephanie was in town, and because his wife was working Stephanie's twin brother Steve spent the day with us. We rode MetroLink to Union Station, saw "Forest Gump," then continued on MetroLink to Laclede's Landing for dinner at The Spaghetti Factory. During the course of the day one of us commented on how long it had been since the four of us -- the twins, Marilyn and I -- had been together for a day.

Waiting for a table at The Spaghetti Factory we walked along the riverfront, enjoying the pleasant July afternoon. Others, couples, families and a few individuals, were scattered along Lenore K. Sullivan Boulevard. As we approached the Arch a family of four, a man, woman and two boys moved past.

The older boy, perhaps six, was holding the hand of his younger brother, who was probably three or four. The man barked at the boy, critical because of something he had let his brother do, warning him not to let it happen again. The child looked frightened, and spoke quietly to his young brother. It was then that I noticed the belt that the man carried looped in his hand.

I felt, rather than heard, Steve's intake of air next to me. I was all too conscious of my own rising emotions: anger, first, and then fear. Or was it the other way around? And then that feeling I have come to know so well, that I have observed so many of the men (and women) I work with experience: the overwhelming frustration I have come to call *helpless obligation.*

My behavioral response was "ambivalent paralysis." The *"protector of lost children"* part of me demanded intervention: protect the mistreated child, confront the offending parent. But the *"afraid of getting hurt"* me held back, said nothing. Or was that the part of me that has wisdom, that recognized that confrontation could threaten violence against me and mine, could even worsen the vise on the child?

I have found it difficult, over the past two months, to put this incident out of my mind. I understand all too well the dilemmas we face in such situations every day, and have long accepted the reality of the "helpless obligation" conditions they precipitate. I can also accept – even tolerate – the fearfulness that too frequently produces secret paralysis. What keeps bothering me is not what happened, or didn't happen, *during* the incident, but that none of us said anything about it *afterward.*

Interestingly, I do not recall thinking about it later that day at the restaurant. It was only days later that it returned to mind, an apt demonstration, I suppose, of the power of denial. If any of the rest of us thought about it, nothing was said. We may all have felt responsible, I suppose, but somehow I think that I should feel more responsible than the others, and, therefore, that I, most of all, let the frightened child down.

I understand that my reaction was what clinically might be termed "countertransference." That, too, is a familiar feeling, experienced every time a parent or parents bring to my office a "problem child" that seems more "scapegoated" than "bad." I too often have had to fight rising anger when a parent complains about his son's hair, or her daughter's friends, or their choice of music.

I contain the anger because I understand that it – the anger – is a product of me, of my own experiences, and it – my anger – does not belong in the clinical process, will not help this family. "Helpless obligation," I have learned, is also an inevitable by-product of doing therapy.

I do sometimes wonder, however, whether I should "recuse" myself (the one new word I learned from the Whitewater hearings) from working with families with scapegoated kids. Or would that simply be another example of the fine art of denial?

And I do wish I had had the courage to bring the subject up with Marilyn, Steve and Stephanie.

Grieving and Jimmy Durante
(December, 1995)

On the Wednesday after we returned from vacation I became ill and, canceling evening appointments, went home. I fell asleep with the television on, and awoke as a movie (which I later realized was *Sleepless in Seattle*) was beginning. *Sleepless in Seattle* begins, even before the credits, with Jimmy Durante singing "As Time Goes By." You may remember Jimmy Durante: seemingly eternally old, with a gravelly voiced "Brooklyn" style that emphasized every syllable, and a humongous schnozzola (to use his favorite term).

"You must re-mem-ber dis," sang Durante, "A kiss is just a kiss/ A sigh is just a sigh/ The fun-da-ment-al tings apply/ As time goes by." Because I did not have my contacts in I still did not know what the movie was, but it did not matter: I was already crying.

Now *Sleepless in Seattle* is a delightful movie, but not one that would ordinarily bring me to tears. Neither would I have normally expected tears from music by Jimmy Durante. But I did understand what was happening.

A few weeks before vacation a very dear friend had died. The first night on vacation I learned of the suicide of a young client. While in San Francisco I visited the grave of my birth father, who I had "found" too late, and visited my developmentally disabled half-sister, who cannot help me know him. And so it is probably not surprising that, awakening from an exhausted sleep and not yet having erected defenses, prompted by Durante's uniquely evocative style, emotions surfaced. What it was, was *grieving*.

Twice in the past week clients in my office have questioned their grieving. The first, a super-macho law enforcement type, had recently lost a brother with whom he had been estranged. For the better part of an hour, with considerable intensity, he talked about his brother. At times he spoke sadly of their estrangement; at times angrily; and at times there was pride as he recounted a story from their youth. Finally he said what was bothering him: he had wanted to cry, but he had been unable to do so.

I told him that I would not be surprised if his tear ducts had not "long since rusted shut" (which may have been humor that played better at that time than it now sounds), but that I was pretty sure that what I had been listening to *was* grieving. The absence of tears, it seems to me, need not invalidate the process.

The second client was a woman who had recently experienced the tragic death of an adult son -- the second son she had lost in similar circumstances. She had, of course, been devastated. There had been tears. There had been rage. But there had not been the *intensity* of response she had experienced when her first son had died. This time she had not fallen apart (at least not yet), had not been overwhelmed and non-functional, a condition that had lasted nearly three years with her first son. She was concerned that something was wrong, that she was "not feeling enough."

But how much is enough? Is there a proper way to grieve? Must we always grieve the same?

At one level these questions are about grieving, and about how we might work best with grieving clients. At another level, they apply to much of what we do as clinicians. I become concerned when therapists become prescriptive, when we think we know *how* a life-process should be done, *what* one should be doing or thinking or feeling. And yet we constantly face pressures to do just that: from the sameness of the problems that parade into our offices, to the demands of managed care that we effect cures in ever-decreasing increments of treatment, to the bankruptcy of our individual creativities as we become more and more exhausted.

But at an even broader level I think the questions may apply to each of us, in our individual lives, as we face universal experiences. *Sleepless in Seattle* was billed as a romantic comedy, but it was first and foremost a story about coping and recovery from loss. Unlike many other stories where one anticipates (or fears) impending catastrophe, *Sleepless* opens with Tom Hanks trying to explain the death of his beloved wife to their son. For much of the film Hanks copes marginally, mired in grief while (the "comedy" aspect of the story) women across the country, and especially Meg Ryan, plot to save him.

Perhaps the end line of *Sleepless in Seattle* – that true love can save even those who have lost perfect love – is contrived, but author Jeff Arch and director Nora Ephron nevertheless make an important point: that loss may be better understood as a *beginning* than as an *ending*.

Loss is, without question, universal. As good therapists know, each of us experiences loss not only in death, but in growth, in change, even in the exciting events of our lives: the birth of a first child also brings a loss of freedom. As I come to terms with losses in my own life I have also come to recognize that a primary purpose of life *is* to come to terms with loss. More and more I see therapy as the process of helping hurting people accept endings, limits, universal life boundaries.

But much as in the ultimate astronomical question – if the universe has a boundary *what's just beyond that point?* – every ending has a "point just beyond." My interest has increasingly been on that "point beyond" for the living, as we *experience* the loss rather than on the loss itself. For the living the point just beyond the loss is *life,* and, ideally, life that incorporates the lost within it. The *process* in that "point" is what we call "grieving."

This is the fundamental issue, I believe, in all spiritual traditions. Life is about limits, about loss. But loss is not about endings; loss is about beginnings. *Loss* means *life.* And *life* is about *hope.* It is still, eternally, true: *The fundamental things apply/ As time goes by.*

The Old Man and the C

(July, 1997)

That's a hard "C," as in "cane."

I've had an opportunity recently to engage in one of those social experiments, similar to the "trust" exercises from the days of sensitivity training, where I could experience what it would be like to be an old man.

Now, some might think this was no experiment. *I* might even say that: by the standards of my youth, at 59 and counting, I *am* old. Still, I will, hopefully, get older yet; and I've had, I'm afraid, a frightening glimpse into what that future might be like.

It all started, as a bad novel might begin, on a dark and stormy March weekend in Boston; and it was fueled by an excess of macho. My wife and her sister are selling the old family home, and we had spent the weekend sorting through pictures, measuring furniture, and clambering through dusty attics. My wife was interested in two paintings of New England scenes, and we decided to carry them back with us on the plane.

Wrapped and bagged it was obvious (at least to my wife) that they were too heavy to carry through two airports, but male socialization (and testosterone, or what testosterone's left at my age) could permit no such "weaseling." We (I) *could* carry the paintings; we (I) *would* carry the paintings; and, therefore, we (I) *did* carry them.

Two days later there was soreness in, to put it politely, my backside. I assumed it would, as always, go away. It did. But it was replaced, within a few days, by spasms shooting the length of my leg that would have, if I could have reached my foot, knocked my sock off.

What I'm saying here is that sciatica *hurts*! It's not easy to get away from a pain that is present whether you sit, stand, walk, or get in or out of a car, or even lie down or get out of bed.

It also turns out to be hard to do a job that requires sitting, when you can't, and listening, when you're distracted by pain. Furthermore, it's hard to do therapy, when you're in pain, with codependent clients who are so concerned with *your* pain that they forget to pay attention to their own.

So I hobbled to Walgreen's for a cane.

It turns out that selecting a cane is not all that easy. They come in differing sizes and colors and are made of different materials, and, naturally, vary greatly in price. They also don't come with directions which, surprisingly, would be helpful. Who would have thought you were supposed to carry the cane in the hand *opposite* the bad leg?

Nevertheless, we finally selected a lovely little number with a huge rubber band inside that permitted it to be folded up and then, like magic, snapped into action. Even on one leg, and doped up on pain killers, little boys must have their fun.

I did learn that using a cane is a mixed blessing. It certainly makes getting around easier, although when you have both arms full (for example, of car-to-office essentials like a briefcase, laptop, lunch, umbrella, and pillow) a cane reduces one's carrying capacity considerably. I did, however, tend to get doors held open for me, especially by attractive young women who wouldn't have noticed me a few days before.

But hobbling around on a cane seems like something an *old man* would do; and the cane (or perhaps the *pain*) tends to produce a stooped and rickety appearance. And then the devilish device produces *its own* aches and pains – in the hand, arm, and shoulder, for example – making the user even more uncomfortable (and crotchety). The result: "instant geezer".

After a few unsuccessful sessions with a chiropractor and the obligatory, but ineffective, round of muscle relaxants I found myself inside an MRI. (Being in an MRI, for the uninitiated, is a little like being inside a coffin, only noisier.) The results disclosed a herniated disc.

The recommended treatment – mid-range between doing nothing and surgery – was a series of epidural steroid injections. These injections (which are themselves remarkably painful), do seem to be helping.

But, unfortunately, they elicit very little sympathy. First, as everyone knows, men don't know how to be empathetic, especially with another man; and second, all women seem to have had epidurals, or childbirth, or both – or know other women who have. When it comes to pain women can always claim the moral high ground.

Suffice it to say that, since the pain is easing, the cane has been returned to its case, and the grand social experiment is over.

Or is it? Perhaps, at 59 and counting, it's just beginning.

Checkers, anyone?

Reaching Out

I was able to escape into the world because I was bright enough to get a scholarship to college. As previously noted, I left home to "study science," primarily because there were more "competency points" in science; but the rest of my life's journey has been marked by steady progress toward service to others.

By "escape" I do not mean to imply that I was held captive, or that my parents did not support my college plans. But these were the fifties, and universal college education, at least for rural farm families, was little more than a dream. Furthermore, we were poor -- not "dirt poor," I suppose, but "cash poor," as all our assets were in mortgaged land. There was no money to send me to college.

I do not know if paying for my education was ever discussed by my parents. They did not share their discussions or money concerns with me. But I do know that money was never offered. I left for Rolla, Missouri, and the Missouri School of Mines, the state's engineering school, with only the few hundred dollars I had raised working and through a Future Farmer's project raising a few calves for market, and a Curator's scholarship worth tuition and a little spending money.

I use the term "escape" to describe getting away from the rural farm environment and, in particular, the oppressive isolation of my own experiences. I would not have long survived had I remained at home.

I was not at Rolla long, however, before my lifelong yearning for "something else" emerged. By the beginning of my junior year (interestingly, just as classes were getting harder) I had decided to become a minister – Baptist, Southern variety, because I had been taken in by Rolla's First Church – and arranged a transfer to Baylor University in Waco, Texas.

From there the progression has continued: after a brief side-step into banking (the only job I could get on arriving in Los Angeles), I worked as a welfare worker, parole officer, work release center supervisor, college teacher and, most recently, as a psychotherapist. In one way or another, service jobs all.

How do I understand this? Not, I'm sorry to say, as obsessive altruism, although there has probably been some altruism involved; nor because of a recognition of requisite skills. I certainly did not possess the social or assertive skills for successful ministry, nor the directive abilities necessary for corrections work. Rather, I think I was *making retribution*, repayment, perhaps for the good fortune of escaping into the world or, more likely, to work away the eternal sense of shame I carried with me.

I have always had ambivalence toward the world, fearing it while yearning to save it. It is, I suppose, some vestigial messianic feeling not yet resolved. Although that ambivalence was nowhere confronted more overtly than when I was a parole officer in California, it has been there throughout. Thus, I was ardently for civil rights, but participated in no marches or demonstrations; I have felt anguish at news of earthquake, bombing or hurricane, but have taken no steps in response; I have observed injustices large and small, and have done little more than murmur concern.

But, of course, that is not totally fair: I have served on church boards too numerous to mention, have worked with and led volunteer activities throughout my life, and have organized my entire professional life, from corrections to college teaching to counseling, more for service than for personal gain.

And, of course, I have reflected on the world – on the people I have met, the work I have done, and the problems around me – and, occasionally, have written those observations down.

Places

Annisquam
(October, 1990)

In August Marilyn and I flew to Boston and drove to Annisquam, a one-time fishing village on Cape Ann about an hour's drive north, where we met Marilyn's sister Martha and her family. Marilyn and Martha grew up in Annisquam, where their parents rented a house each summer.

We stayed at the Brynmere, a 100 year old hotel now operating as a bed-and-breakfast during the summer months. The Brynmere sits one house away from Cambridge Beach, a small, sandy (at low tide), rocky spot where the Annisquam River opens into Ipswich Bay. Around the corner you can see Annisquam Light, a picture-perfect lighthouse that marks the entrance to the River, and from there a back entrance through "The Cut" (a canal) to Gloucester Harbor.

Although Cambridge Beach faces west toward New Hampshire and Maine, Annisquam is actually well out into the Atlantic. Boats – sailboats, yachts, even a few remaining fishing boats – go in and out daily. It is a spot where the sound of a motor is more likely to be a boat than a car or an airplane. It is a peaceful village, apparently forgotten by time.

People seem to live a long time in Annisquam. A few years ago I met Mrs. Clark, who rented a house to Marilyn's family when Marilyn was young. Mrs. Clark was 101 years old when I met her, living at home, and sharp as a tack. Now 104, she lives in a nursing home.

Each time we go to Annisquam we visit Martha Gladding, about 85, a life-long friend of the family. Martha Gladding always tells me how handsome I am. I like Martha Gladding.

Perhaps people live a long time in Annisquam because of the terrain. Situated on rocky bluffs and hills, the area was once the site of productive granite quarrying. Two-and three-story houses lie across steep hillsides, each seeking a view of the water. House colors are bold: some white with bright trims, but others deep shades of brown, or gray, or red. Not far north on Highway 127 is a bright pink church with a jarring purple door.

There are many interesting things one can do on Cape Ann, including seeing Bearskin Neck at Rockport, an artists' community; or Gloucester, where the famous "Old Man of the Sea" statue commemorates the fishing industry; or the Hammond Castle, a private residence build like a medieval castle. You can take tram tours, boat trips around the Cape, even a "whale-sighting" cruise.

Mostly, though, you do nothing in Annisquam: sit on the beach or (if the tide is in) on an "elephant" rock; sit on the breezy porch at the Inn; take a walk; or if you are young and adventurous, climb "Squam Rock," a huge boulder protruding out of the highest hill in town.

The most interesting part of the vacation for me, however, was being with Marilyn and Martha as they re-experienced their youth. On walks they would talk about each house: who had lived there, what had happened to them, and how the house had changed. At the beach they would meet people they knew when they were young (and who came each day for a dip in the ice-cold water), or the sons and daughters of people they grew up with. On the porch they shared memories, filling in the crevices of each other's experiences.

On a Thursday evening walk we came upon the Annisquam Historical Society, open only Monday and Thursday evenings, with countless pictures and artifacts, including nine volumes of picture postcards alone. What was fascinating about all of this was not the information; genealogies of people I've never known are not particularly exciting. I found myself caught up in the process: the merging of memories, the sharing of lives.

Somehow, surprisingly, watching this also brought sadness. I found myself envying those experiences, that sharing. I have no brothers or sisters; and my family engaged in few of the regular experiences that produce such memories. I could not tell you who lived in houses in the small town near where I grew up; or even, for that matter, on neighboring farms.

Deprived childhood? Perhaps; but this is not an essay on deprivation. We are what we have lived, and I have gained from solitary as well. This is, really, nothing more than an observation about how memories and places and families can intersect and produce something valuable and exciting.

I'm glad I was there. I learned something about Marilyn's family, and I learned something about being-in-family.

Annisquam is, indeed, a special place.

The Coming of Morning at Lost Valley Lake
(March, 1992)

I called my mother early the other morning, to see how my father, who was in the hospital, was doing and to see how she was holding up. She sounded drained, and was worried about Dad. He was on oxygen, and surgery was being discussed.

She insisted, nevertheless, that she was "fine," even though she had been awake since 4:30 AM. Not being able to sleep, she had "done a few things:" a load of laundry (sheets); some cooking (two chickens, in anticipation of Dad's return); and "a little cleaning" (scrubbing down part of a wall). "It's better when I keep busy," she insisted.

"Lost Valley" sounds like a Hollywood remake of Shangri-La, but in fact it is a family resort about 75 miles west of St. Louis. Close enough to get to easily, it is still far enough for one to feel as if he or she has gotten away. There is much to do at Lost Valley: a small lake with swimming, boating and fishing; a Lodge and Sports Arena with sports, games and movies; hills, trees and walking paths; horses to ride; and accommodations ranging from tents to condos.

The man had gone to Lost Valley for the weekend, however, to do nothing, or as close to nothing as possible. And so it came to be that, unable to sleep, the man sat on the deck of his condo and watched morning come over Lost Valley Lake.

As the sky slipped from darkness toward light he wished for the gift of art, for the ability to somehow capture the experience. If he were an artist, he thought, he could paint the early eastern sky tinged with shades of red and blue; or the half-moon shining brightly high in the western sky. Or he might picture the unbroken sheen of the surface of the lake, marked only with the reflections of trees lining the hills on the opposite shore.

With the gift of art, he thought, he could record the repetitive refrain of a lone early bird, punctuated by squawking of distant geese, which gradually gave way to the sounds of more birds singing; to the drumming echo of a woodpecker from across the lake; and to the calls of crows beginning their day.

As morning progressed the man watched, marveling, shivering in the early spring chill. Gradually, the eastern vista brightened, colors softening to pastel, while the moon became pale, ephemeral. The sky overhead grew blue, sprinkled with wisps of cotton-candy clouds. A chimney of steam, rising from the lodge, flattened into a ceiling of haze above the western lake shore. And the trees on the opposite shore began to take individual shape as new light shone through and separated their still leafless branches.

As the man watched the first hint of sun peeked over the eastern shore and rose into a bright yellow globe, fringed with a halo of reds and oranges. The earlier sounds of silence marred only by birds gave way to rumbles of distant trucks. A car passed. The night had transformed itself to day.

The man rose and went back into the apartment, and into the still dark bedroom. He got in bed, comforted by sound of breathing from his still-sleeping wife, and reflected on the ordinary miracle he had witnessed. Morning had come again, an event as timeless as eternity, as majestic as the eternal.

As the weekend ended I talked to my mother again. Dad was now home, free from the hospital but still tethered to oxygen. As my mother described the things she was doing I realized again how much she feared stillness, and how much of that fear I carried within myself.

And as the week progressed, and as I encountered again the crises with which I occupy my working week, I yearned anew for the stillness of the lake; and for the chance to once again witness the coming of morning at Lost Valley Lake.

Summer in Iowa
(September, 2000)

When I was a student at the Missouri School of Mines and Metallurgy (since renamed the University of Missouri - Rolla), a hundred years or so ago, I recall a cartoon displaying a "hayseed" and captioned, "Six months ago I couldn't even spell 'Injuneer;' and now I are one!"

I thought of that cartoon years later, when I was retooling from college teacher to private-practice psychologist. Of course, there were differences: I had been a card-carrying member of APA for years and, usually, I could actually spell "psychologist."

But I knew I didn't know much about *being* a psychologist out in the world of helping people. Since, with one or two exceptions, I didn't even know any "practicing" psychologists, I had no clear idea how to look or act. So, in a daring move that made sense at the time, I began attending meetings of the St. Louis Psychological Association. The next thing I knew, I was Treasurer.

One thing about the modern era: change comes faster and faster. Career and lifestyle choices, which once could be expected to last a lifetime, now barely survive a decade or two. And so, less than twenty years later, I'm "retooling" again, not so much *giving up* being a psychologist as *adding* the identity of "writer". And, once again, familiar questions arise: what, exactly does a writer look like? How does he or she do whatever it is that he or she does? Where does one go to get to know real writers?

Of course, writers are everywhere but, much like private-practice psychologists, they tend to do their work in solitary settings. And since, surprisingly, they look pretty much like ordinary people, they're hard to spot in a crowd.

What you have to do, it turns out, is go to Iowa. As strange as it may seem, they raise writers as well as corn in Iowa. Who knew?

Now, it isn't that I have had anything *against* Iowa. It's just that I had never actually *been* there. Until this summer.

Iowa City, the home of the University of Iowa and the world-famous Iowa Summer Writer's Festival is a surprisingly pleasant spot in the southeastern part of the state. The original state capital, Iowa City spreads along both sides of the meandering Iowa River.

With a population of about 60,000, it is host to more than 20,000 students in a university that is so integrated into the community it is impossible to tell where one leaves off and the other begins. A stroll from the student union, on the river, past the old capital into downtown is five or six blocks (although up a mean hill).

I spent a week in Iowa City this July, attending two workshops. I learned a lot of "writer stuff," although I must say that it's hard *not* to learn when you start out knowing nothing. For example, I learned that the noun "workshop" can also be a verb, as in "I 'workshopped' – subjected writing to critical review by other workshop participants – two stories this week." I also learned that I could survive having stories that *I* thought were pretty good "workshopped."

And then, of course, there was serious, even useful, information: a workshop on "plot and structure," led by Susan Taylor Chehak, a delightful storyteller who's most recent novel, *Smithereens*, has been described as "Midwestern Gothic;" and "short fiction for publication," led by Mark Jude Poirier, who's first collection of stories is *Naked Pueblo: Stories.* Plus, lectures by Leigh Michaels, author of more than 60 romance novels; Susan Chehak, on "the art of lying;" and Nancy Barry, on writing essays for radio.

Ultimately, though, the most valuable part of the Iowa experience was spending a week in the midst of several hundred people serious about writing, with the opportunity to get to know one or two dozen through reading their work and listening to their observations about my work. It was affirming, validating, and invigorating: that is, the stuff of which *identity* is made.

Which was, come to think of it, the reason I went to Iowa in the first place.

Each year, the Festival sponsors produce a "logo," imprinted on tee shirts and book bags. As an enrollee in two workshops I was given one of each. This year's image is a clothesline full of laundry and, on the bright red tee, was emblazoned in white. As a proud "workshopper" (remember, it's a verb now!), I've been wearing my shirt often. But I *have* noticed curious looks by others, no doubt non-writers, who seem to be wondering why I am wearing laundry.

Yes, in addition to everything else, I've finally learned what a writer *looks* like!

Calhoun
(May, 2001)

On the fateful day, the day of decision, we headed west, into St. Charles County, on our way to Illinois.

"Well, now," I can hear you thinking, "there's a problem here. Illinois is *east* of St. Louis, not west."

Au contraire, my geographically challenged friends: large portions of Illinois – some would say the most beautiful portions unless you are fanciers of corn – lie *west* of St. Louis. Included in that description, on both counts, is Calhoun County.

If you paid attention to the census results recently summarized in *Post-Dispatch* articles, you may have noted an anomaly. The articles included maps of the St. Louis Standard Metropolitan Statistical Area, the 11 county region that includes and surrounds the city of St. Louis. What was curious, on each map, was the white area at the top-center, between Lincoln County, Missouri and Jersey County, Illinois. One might think that it represented one of the Great Lakes, cut free of its bearings and drifted south. But no. Turns out, that is Calhoun County.

Although clearly within the St. Louis SMSA geographically, Calhoun County, Illinois, is omitted from all computations. It is as if it has been forgotten, lost. Even *Illinois'* officials seldom include it in tabulations.

The reason, I think, is because SMSA's are defined as "counties surrounding and integrated into the economy of a major city." Calhoun may *surround*, but it certainly is not *integrated*.

But it is remarkably beautiful, the delta created by the coming together, at Grafton, Illinois, of the Illinois River (flowing more-or-less straight south from Peoria and above) and the Mississippi (actually flowing *eastward* along a portion of Calhoun County). Almost entirely rural, Calhoun consists of winding roads, rolling hills, and acres of farmland and orchards.

Known locally, for some reason, as "The Kingdom," access to southern Calhoun County is primarily by ferry -- the Golden Eagle, crossing the Mississippi from northern St. Charles County, and the Brussels Ferry, crossing the Illinois near Pere Marquette State Park.

We discovered Calhoun County somewhat by accident, overhearing a friend talk about property he was considering on a bluff overlooking the Mississippi. Curious, and interested in trying the Golden Eagle Ferry, we decided to visit Winneberg.

Winneberg is, today, a villa and single-family home development overlooking the Mississippi a few hundred yards upstream from the ferry crossing; but a hundred years ago it was an industrial settlement, the site of a brick factory and village situated along the river. The villas being planned sit on a rock cliff some 300 feet above the river, looking south toward St. Peters. Seemingly totally isolated, they are only about ten miles from Mid-Rivers' Mall, and less than 30 miles from Clayton.

Of course, that includes a few hundred yards by ferry. Cost aside (round trips are $8.00, with no frequent-crosser discounts; when you have a monopoly you don't have to negotiate), there are periods when the ferry cannot run. Floods, for example, usually amounting to a few days in the spring; or severe winter weather, when the river is frozen. During such times one can cross further north, by bridge, into Jersey County, Illinois.

It's hard to imagine a more dramatic vista, especially so close to the city, for a price that ordinary folk can afford. You can see the stars from Calhoun County -- although we're told that the most dramatic night view is the "city lights."

We'll be finding out, in a few months. They've already started on our villa. Our plans are to relocate there, in a place where we can continue our St. Louis' lives; where Marilyn can come to terms with retirement and I can continue to work a few days a week.

And, of course, to reading and writing. I'm looking forward to sitting on the deck, reading (*Huckleberry Finn* seems natural as a starter), watching Old Man River roll by and, laptop in hand, waxing poetic. And, yes, you're invited to visit. It's only a short fun-filled ferry ride away.

Unless the river is flooded. But, even then, we can keep in touch. They *do* have telephone service in Calhoun County.

First Night
(December, 2001)

A person ought to approach a first night in a new house much as he or she would a first night with a new lover: with high expectations, certainly, but also with care. You can never be sure how things will go. You might decide to leave before the evening is out; or perhaps to steal away before dawn. If things go well, on the other hand, you may linger well into the morning, enjoying, if you will, a second cup of coffee.

Too often, of course, first nights involve little planning, occurring more or less by happenstance. In the case of a house, for example, one may have left himself or herself with nowhere else to go: his or her previous house has been sold, or the apartment lease is up. Just as with a new lover, too often a man or woman moves in precipitously only, years later, to wonder why.

I thought about all of this a few weeks ago as we prepared for our first "sleepover" in our new river house. On a bluff above the Mississippi in Calhoun County, Illinois, our new villa features spectacular vistas: broad expanses of river-view windows, several bays, and a deck directly over the water. But it is isolated. Calhoun County, although close in miles, is as rural as the metro area is, well, metropolitan.

For one thing, it's dark out there at night. Of course, the row of lights dotting the St. Charles County horizon, across the river to the south, *is* enthralling. And there *are* occasional lights from a passing boat or barge; and a regular pattern of blinking lights from airplanes heading east into Lambert.

But immediately around the house nothing is visible. Only memory assures the continued presence of the river; and trees, known to be across the street, vanish into the night's darkness. Except, of course, for the stars. Who knew there were so many stars?

And in addition to being dark in the country at night, it's noisy. Oh, by city standards, it's deathly quiet. But this is the kind of quiet in which *frogs* are deafening. With ambient noises reduced the nighttime sounds of a river tug or airplane are vivid and clear. (Curiously, there are also trains: a track runs along the river on the Missouri side, carrying trainloads of coal or grain west every hour or two.) Boats, trains and planes: only *automobiles* are seldom-heard nighttime sounds in Calhoun County

And so we prepared for our first night at Winneberg. We had entertained friends during the afternoon and evening, marveling at the ever-varying riverfront tableau before us. Changing patterns of light constantly alter a river: blue waters sparkling in the afternoon sun, darkening as the western sky reddens at sundown, becoming black as night descends and distant lights begin to wink.

Dinner was delicious, although something of an adventure: a new stove with too many red lights and obtuse directions. The conversation was pleasant, and the evening wore well. But eventually the stereo, programmed for "random selection," exhausted all five compact discs and turned itself off, and our guests headed back to the ferry and St. Charles' civilization. It was time to face the night.

If it is dark outside beside the river at night, it is even darker inside, especially in a new house where one cannot rely on memory to locate essential places, like the bathroom. Even without window treatments – as far as I know, fish have little interest in a pudgy psychologist's nocturnal habits – there was no ambient light, and we had, naturally, neglected to bring a night light.

Of course, if it is dark at night, it becomes light early enough, and without blinds one is sure to be awake in time to see the surprisingly beautiful sunrise. Below reddening eastern skies the river's outline slowly emerges, gradually distinguishing itself from the opposite bank. Then, suddenly, as the sun peeks above the horizon, sparkling jewels begin to dance across the water.

You will be happy to know that we did stay through the night. In fact, we lingered into the morning for a second cup of coffee, and even a third.

I sat for a while on the deck, watching an early-morning barge chug upstream, reading a bit of Mark Twain's *Life on the Mississippi*. I even allowed myself a momentary smile of pleasure.

This relationship just may work out.

Basement Legacy
(December, 2003)

Shortly after moving to Calhoun County a few months ago we entertained dinner guests. The conversation included "moving discoveries" – things unearthed in the process of changing homes.

"We have these two violins," I commented, "that were buried in the basement of our in-town house. We're trying to figure out what to do with them."

Both of the violins had been rescued from our mothers' houses when they moved into nursing homes; and both were carted to our basement and forgotten. My wife recalls using her mother's violin when she took lessons in high school. My (vague) recollection was that my mother had also played in high school.

And so it was that the four of us gathered in our new basement, where I retrieved the two violins. The first, from Marilyn's mother, was better looking: richer, with a nice grain and good finish. *My* mother's violin looked . . . well, *cheap*.

Our dinner guest, who knew a little about such things, turned the nicer-looking violin this way and that, and even peered into the curved opening in the front. "Sometimes the maker signs his work on the inside," she said; "but I don't see anything in this one."

Peering into the opening of the second violin she squinted, shifting the instrument to catch the light of the hanging bare bulb. "Something is printed in here," she said. "I see what looks like a 'T.' Let's see . . . looks like T - O – N – I – V - S." She pronounced each letter separately. "Then there's another word: S – T – R – A - D . . . ."

The full script, stenciled onto the base and carefully read with the aid of a flashlight, was:

Antonivs Stradiuarivs Cremonensis
Faciebat Anno 1719

Antonio Stradivari was born in 1644 near Cremona, Italy. At about 14 he was apprenticed to Niccolo Amati, a master violin maker. Within a few years he began producing his own instruments. Stradivari, who is known to have made at least 1,116 instruments, including some 540 violins, 12 violas and 50 cellos, did his best work from about 1700 to 1725. His genius lay in careful craftsmanship: interiors and exteriors remarkable in their precision. He also fixed the shape and position of the violin's sound-holes and bridge to produce the best quality of sound.

The very name, "Stradivari," designates the best in violins, and many of his instruments continue to be played today

Life provides far more questions than answers, of course. Was this battered violin, salvaged from my mother's closet, what it appeared to be? If so, how could my mother, a depression-era child, have come upon it? For that matter, did she have any idea what she had?

I did recall Mother once commenting that her violin "might be valuable," so perhaps she did know. But if so, where did it come from? Many questions, but few answers: Mother, currently residing in Bethesda Dilworth's Alzheimer's unit, isn't going to be able to help.

Of course, Mother was part of a larger, talented family. One of my relatives is Rabbi James Stone Goodman (Mother's maiden name was Stone), who's great-great grandfather was my great-grandfather's brother. Goodman, a talented musician, likes to say that everyone in his family "either became a musician or a Rabbi." Goodman turned out to be both, of course, but somehow the musical gene skipped my branch of the family.

So I couldn't help but let my imagination run. What if a *really good* violin came into the family's hands in Poland? Suppose it was passed down from one family member to another, and finally carried to America when family members emigrated in the early 1900s. It *could* have ended up in my basement, couldn't it?

Wouldn't *that* be a legacy for an old woman with Alzheimer's?

It isn't a real "Strad," of course. We showed the two violins to a friend, Janet Boyer, who for years sold classical and folk instruments as the owner of "Music Folk" in Kirkwood. Janet examined both violins carefully, even managing to extract a little sound with one of the old bows.

Marilyn's mother's violin had a nice sound, and would be "a good student violin," Janet said. My mother's violin was most certainly *not* a Stradivari. "You'd be amazed how many fake Strads are out there," Janet said. Apparently, putting the label of a famous instrument-maker in a violin has long been common.

Well, so much for imagination. Or, for that matter, for legacies. Still, in the end, aren't the most important family legacies really *stories*? There *are* stories here, even if Mother can't share them.

For that matter, why can't legacies be questions?

Therapy Lessons

Wounded Healers
(January, 1989)

The lead article by Thomas Maeder in the January, 1989 issue of *The Atlantic,* on "Wounded Healers," deserves – perhaps demands – the full attention of every mental health professional.

Maeder's thesis is that the "helping professions," such as psychotherapy and the ministry, attract more than their share of the "emotionally unstable". He briefly considers the notion that all psychotherapists are "crazy" ("Psychiatrists say that analysts are crazy. Analysts say that psychiatrists are crazy. Both of them say that social workers and psychologists are crazy"); but, other than some evidence of higher suicide rates, Maeder concludes there is no evidence of a higher rate of pervasive gross psychopathology among these groups than the general population.

Yet he does suggest that persons choosing psychotherapy professions may have underlying characteristics that may create problems for the people they treat. For example, he argues, many were cast in childhood roles of family nurturer and later used their work as a way to compensate for what were lonely, unhappy childhoods. Maeder calls such persons "wounded healers", a concept with ancient roots in mythology and religion (St. Paul and St. Augustine, for example).

The danger occurs when the wounded healer has not resolved, or cannot control, his own problems. This may lead to "using the profession as a means of avoiding the need to deal with his problems." Maeder notes that the private practice of psychotherapy is uniquely autonomous, and therapists may therefore suffer from what Ernest Jones has called "The God Complex". Clinically, he suggests, many therapists act out of a narcissistic personality pattern, and may not have been able to experience the kinds of long-term relationships or friendships that enable growth and maturity. The result may be therapists living "vicariously through their patients," in "therapeutic situations [which offer] an unparalleled opportunity for asymmetrical intimacy."

These are serious charges, exacerbated because they appear in a respected publication with national distribution. At the very least, this article represents serious negative public relations for the mental health profession. While one can argue that the charges are biased or undocumented (for example, many assertions are unreferenced), to use this argument to reject the charges would be short-sighted. They deserve serious consideration, I believe, for we know that they are not totally without foundation.

Our questions, as psychotherapists, should be, "How valid are these concerns?" and "What can we do to respond to them?" To whatever degree Maeder's concerns are valid, attention must be directed to the processes by which therapists, of whatever discipline, become credentialed; and to the resources and expectations for continuing growth, development and self-care for therapists.

Thus, requiring that persons preparing to be therapists undergo therapy themselves, as psychoanalysis traditionally has required, may be reasonable. Furthermore, providing resources to motivate working therapists to grow professionally, such as through continuing education or peer or professional supervision, would also be valuable.

Whatever one's view about such suggestions, the questions raised by Thomas Maeder deserve reflection and discussion among serious-minded mental health professionals.

Healing the Wounded Healer
(September, 1995)

Although these reflections were precipitated by the recent suicide of a popular local minister they are not intended to be a commentary on suicide. Neither are they about the theological or moral implications of that individual's actions, despite the tendency of the media and, apparently, many local church leaders, to pronounce judgment. Finally, and in particular, they are not about the Rev. Timothy Brewer himself (whom I did not know).

Rev. Brewer's death brought to mind the concept "wounded healers" from Thomas Maeder's 1989 Atlantic article (Vol. 263; Jan. 1989; pp. 37-47). Maeder was addressing the potential for abuse by emotionally unstable psychotherapists or clergypersons who use their clients or parishioners to meet their own narcissistic needs.

Such persons too often grow up believing that hard work and responsibility are the only things that give them value in others' eyes. They have a chronically low sense of self-worth and a stunted ability to receive genuine love or friendship from others. Only their selfishly selfless labors make them feel satisfied with themselves. As a result, they may be driven into helping motivated not by altruism but by a desperate need to fill an inner vacancy -- an effort that ultimately helps very little, because it can never succeed until they have attended to the necessary repairs.

I have no idea if such narcissism described Rev. Brewer, but I suspect it describes, to some degree, many of us "healers," whether clergy or therapists. Psychotherapy and the ministry are natural venues for persons seeking self-definition from their work, from others in their lives.

To some degree, of course, all professional helpers seek value from their roles; that, in itself, does not define any of them as narcissistic. And in a larger sense anyone may find him- or herself in a helper, caretaker, role. So the question may apply to any of us: where do we go, what do we do, when we are "wounded?" Where do "wounded healers" go for help?

Several years ago, when my father died, I canceled appointments for a few days while in southwestern Missouri for my father's final hours and to tend to my mother's immediate needs. Upon returning to St. Louis I immediately resumed my regular schedule. After all, I reasoned, I could do nothing at home, and "these people needed me." In truth, I was using work to avoid issues and feelings that were too uncomfortable to confront.

Of course, one of the first persons I saw upon returning needed to talk about the death of her father. I found myself in a jumble of confused thoughts and feelings. Upon reflection, I realize that I should not have presumed that I could be helpful without first beginning to deal with my personal issues.

There are other factors that may prevent us from seeking help, such as a need to be perfect, or a belief that we cannot bring our problems to anyone in our own community. These are variations on the same theme: "How can I help anyone else if I have problems myself?" "How can I admit to anyone else (especially a colleague!) that I cannot solve my own problems?"

And, of course, if we are really committed caregivers we should want to serve, never be concerned about money or time or personal issues, and never ever feel angry or put upon or used. (And God forbid that we might feel attracted to -- or repelled by -- a client!)

So what can we do if we do feel any of these things? What if we feel helpless in the face of the overwhelming problems brought to us? What if we feel helpless in the face of our own problems? Where does the wounded healer take his or her wounds?

What we cannot do is what is most likely: to deny that we hurt, to rationalize or to minimize the issues or problems at hand. The risk of denial is precisely because we have accepted the irrational belief that we should not -- could not -- have problems.

So the necessary first step is acceptance: recognition that the knot in the pit of our stomach is anxiety, that our growing tenseness and cognitive confusion is anger. With such acceptance we can begin to separate our own issues from those brought into our offices. In doing this, of course, we are doing nothing more than what we encourage our clients to do.

Where more help is needed we have access to other resources: supervision (more available for therapists than clergy) and/or therapy. (Of course we can rely upon the confidentiality of good therapists and supervisors. Could they not rely upon us?)

As therapists, or clergy, we carry a sacred trust -- not because of who we are but because of our roles. We violate that trust if – intentionally or unintentionally – we use our clients to meet our own needs.

There is no sin in being wounded. We only sin when we fail to attend to our own wounds before making worse the wounds of others.

Revisiting Miri's Woods
(January, 1996)

I've told the story previously of the small wooded area a few blocks from our home that my granddaughter Miriam and I "discovered." "Miriam's Woods" was about trying to see the world through the eyes of a child, about how a small patch of trees and a creek could be an adventure, and about a child and grandparent getting to know each other. It was, I thought, a good story, warm and loving.

I did, however, omit part of the story. I left the ending out, rationalized at the time as "not relevant." Actually, truthfully, I did not include the ending because it was embarrassing, and because, at the time, I wasn't clear about what had happened.

It's time to tell "the rest of the story" (with apologies to Paul Harvey), even though it is still embarrassing, because I'm beginning to understand and because what happened *does* have relevance. In the process I may open a "can of worms," that may leave some readers uncomfortable, and may leave few "ungored oxen" (to misuse an old expression).

Miriam was about four when we visited the wooded area she had found with her mother. As I recall it was late fall and rather cool, so we were wearing warmer clothing. After some wandering among the trees and a few minutes scaring Granddad to death climbing onto a fallen log overlooking the creek below Miriam announced, as one might have anticipated, that she had to "go potty . . . now!"

We were alone in the woods. I clearly understood that the reasonable thing to do, and certainly the thing I would have done when my children were young, would have been to pull down her pants and let her urinate among the trees (probably adding to her sense of "adventure"). But I could not bring myself to do the reasonable thing.

I couldn't do that because it was, somehow, too uncomfortable. Instead, I began hurrying home (three or four blocks, but uphill), and because Miriam couldn't walk fast enough and hold herself at the same time I carried her, damn near giving myself a heart attack in the process. When we got home, of course, I had to pull down her pants anyway, so she could go to the toilet.

It was not clear to me, at the time, what was uncomfortable about "the reasonable thing." I had no reason to believe that my daughter, who had entrusted Miriam to my care, would be offended with her daughter's "peeing in the woods" (which is, of course, what Anne told me – after Miri told her – *she* would have done had she been there). It was certainly the appropriate thing to do, and far more desirable than wet pants or cardiac arrest.

Recently we entertained two of our daughters-in-law (who are sisters) and their mother, who gathered in St. Louis from Tennessee, Kansas and Southern Illinois to shop and schmooze. Our daughters-in-law's mother, Linda, is a retired school teacher, a warm and loving woman. At one point she asked me if I had seen the recent PBS report on therapists who, as she put it, "make money encouraging patients to recover false memories" of childhood abuse.

I had seen only the last few minutes of the report but I could tell Linda that I, too, was concerned. In fact, I told Linda, I was currently participating in the Missouri Task Force on Responsible Psychotherapy, established to respond to such concerns. I also told Linda that I did not think the problem was greed as much as well-intentioned therapists causing harm in misguided attempts to heal.

I'm not sure Linda was comforted. Neither are any number of other observers, including practitioners, researchers, clients, and family members of clients. With due respect to clinicians worried about the dangers of managed care, there are those who suggest that the biggest threat to psychotherapy today lies in uninformed practice methods that too often may be harmful, if not actually abusive.

At the very least our professional credibility is at stake. When licensed, and presumably representative, mental health professionals advertise "past-life regression therapy," or build practice specialties based on unproven and/or clearly inaccurate concepts about memory, or diagnose on the basis of check lists of symptoms – and then treat (and cure!) the very disorders they have created with these "diagnoses" -- we are all impacted.

Is there a relationship between my woodlands discomfort and this controversy over repressed/false memory? Of course there is. Both are expressions of our current cultural angst about childhood child abuse. Have no doubt: we *must* be concerned about child abuse. But we must also be concerned about over-reacting, condoning, or even promoting abuse through inaccurate accusations.

A psychiatrist friend, also on the Task Force, recently reminded me of the Hippocratic Oath: "First do no harm." "Of course," I noted, "psychologists and other mental health workers don't take the Hippocratic Oath."

Perhaps, she suggested, we should.

Coming to Terms with "The Question"
(October, 1996)

It was one of those damnably frustrating telephone conversations with a managed care case reviewer. She caught me in the ten minutes between clients, intent on challenging every detail of a reauthorization request, and repeatedly asked for specificity and quantification of symptoms (*i.e.,* behavioral documentation).

I objected, arguing that focusing on such data would change the nature of the therapy when she innocently asked, "But then, if you have no quantifiable data, how do you know if you're doing a good job?"

The question stunned and then infuriated me. What impudence! How could this young case reviewer of unknown credentials and uncertain experience consider lecturing me on how to do therapy! Here I was, "busting my tail," filling out endless forms just to have the privilege of serving one of her referrals -- and at $25 off my regular fee at that -- and she had the audacity to imply that I didn't know what I was doing!

Of course, what made things particularly difficult was that under it all, in my heart of hearts, I knew that it was a good question, an absolutely essential question, and -- when push came to shove -- one I wasn't sure I knew how to answer.

Despite initial appearances this is *not* intended to be a diatribe against managed care. Readers of these pages may recognize that I am a realist and a conciliator: I always try to find a way to come to terms with the world as it actually is. Thus, I have always suggested that we look for ways to work with managed care, to try to resolve the inevitable difficulties and abuses as mental health financing transitions into more controlled models. Toward that end I personally have several managed care contracts, have worked to develop skills translating what I do as a therapist into "behavior-speak," and have positive relationships with several managed care referral and review sources.

This is not to say that I do not have serious concerns. Managed care, by definition, lays waste to time-honored concepts of confidentiality. One major company, carrying this problem to its logical end, even manages the care provided to *its own employees,* thus making it impossible for a service provider to be very honest in attempting to justify additional services.

Another company, apparently having grown much too fast, has repeatedly had to ask *us* for information on clients they have referred because they can find nothing in their computers. And too many, as documented above, appear to misunderstand the distinction between a *reviewer* of services and a *supervisor* of services.

But these problems -- serious though they are -- will resolve themselves with time. We are, as previously noted, in a transitional period. I am quite sure that mental health service delivery in the future will look quite different that it has in the past; but I am equally sure that our human quest for excellence will impact the services of the future.

And when it does "the question" -- *how do you know you're doing a good job?* -- will still be there, still relevant, still difficult to answer.

I *did* try to answer the impudent case reviewer, of course. After a moment's hesitation the old "silver-tongued devil" said, glibly, "Because my clients get better. They tell me that they are pleased. They send their friends to me." My answer served the immediate purpose, I suppose, in that the case reviewer changed the subject. Still, in my "heart of hearts," *I* knew that I had evaded the question.

We are dealing with pretty complex and subjective stuff when we're tinkering with people's lives, their happiness, or their relationships. Clearly, the whole of human existence is much more than the sum of its parts. There are intangible realities of life that we cannot measure, can only know in the abstract. *Any* attempt to quantify what we do inevitably minimizes the results, losing something intangible but essential.

In the end observations of progress, customer satisfaction, or even continued referrals can do no more than suggest that our work is good. All of us know of instances where our best work only resulted in disappointed clients, continued dysfunction or broken marriages.

And yet most of us are constantly striving to improve our efforts, to find better ways to help others. What knowledge, what experience, what ideas inform those efforts?

There is irony here: in the context of saving money the question of how one knows one is doing good work may seem unfair; but in the context of the struggle to serve people in pain it is absolutely essential. And if you and I are not involved in trying to find the answers somebody else, with less pure motives, will do it for us.

For an "unfair" question it turns out that there is a lot at stake in the answer.

The Price of Power
(March, 1997)

I have always been uncomfortable with power.

I recognize the irony here: I have always possessed power, whether I wanted it or not or, for that matter, whether I exercised it. I am male, and a white male at that. I have also held some of the most powerful jobs in existence. I have, after all, been a parole officer, a college teacher, and a psychotherapist.

I have been intrigued, and repelled, by power – especially *my* power – since I learned that parolees I supervised in Los Angeles in the 1960s (most of whom intimidated *me*) referred to me behind my back as "Jesus Christ" (as in, "I can't do nothin' with you tonight, man. I've got to stay home -- J C is coming around.") The appellation, which was applied to parole agents in general and not to me alone, referred to power, not spirituality. We had the power, largely unchecked by supervision or review, to provide or withdraw freedom: to release someone from prison or send him back for nothing more serious than "failure to cooperate."

As I have passed through succeeding careers I have found myself reflecting again and again about the exercise (or abuse) of such power. A parole officer's power over his or her caseload is raw and direct. By contrast, a college teacher exercises power that seems narrower, limited to the grading function. One course – two or three credits – would not seem to be the end of the earth. But, of course, to a frightened student it can be. Scholarships, parental support, or entrance into graduate school, to say nothing about self-esteem, can all be perceived to rest on the scoring of a single answer on a test.

I still recall the brilliant but uncooperative graduate student at Virginia Commonwealth University who was dropped from our program in part because he made a "D" in my course on Criminal Justice Systems. He made a "D," largely, because he insisted on writing his final examination in nearly illegible handwriting with a soft red felt-tipped pen. I had told him, after laboring over his mid-term for hours, that I would not grade his final if he presented it in the same fashion. Of course the faculty did not want to claim him as a graduate, but, on reflection, there must have been a better solution.

I have never had a more powerful role, I think, than that of psychotherapist. But it is without question the most subtle: in the guise of helping our clients develop their own selves *we* define the standards to which they implicitly recognize they should aspire. There is yet another irony here, for most good psychotherapists bear power with discomfort; and too many deny its existence, deluding themselves, and their clients as well, that the therapy relationship is egalitarian.

It is not, and can never be. The very fact that one, the client, comes to another, the therapist, for help, and *pays* for that help, *defines* a power differential. We are most likely to get in trouble when we forget this fundamental fact, as Marilyn Peterson has so eloquently pointed out in *At Personal Risk: Boundary Violations in Professional-Client Relationships* (Norton, 1992).

Which is why I think we all should pay attention to a recent story out of Springfield, Missouri (reported in the *Post-Dispatch* on November 18, 1996), of a one million dollar settlement of a lawsuit against a church and church counselor who had helped an Oklahoma woman "recover" memories of childhood abuse. It is too simple to avoid the issue by suggesting that the church counselor did not know what she was doing, or that she had an "ax" to grind. First, we do not know that; and second, each of us has had the experience of an intuitive understanding of a client's presenting problem, often after an all-too-brief conversation, with the resulting conviction that we knew just what was needed to help.

This happens most readily when the client's stories seem to fit a frame of reference (*i.e.,* theory) we hold dear. The danger is that we then "fit" the rest of the facts into *our* frame, and define the client, and the client's treatment, to meet *our* needs. That is, according to Marilyn Peterson, a recipe for therapeutic abuse.

To reduce the risk we must a) recognize and "own" the power we possess in the therapeutic relationship; and b) operate with humility recognizing that all our training, and all our experiences *best* prepares us to understand our limits: that we *do not know everything* and, in fact, *may not know anything* about what to do with this person sitting in our office with us.

Only then, I fear, can we responsibly exercise the power we hold as therapists.

Public Lessons

Deja Vu in L.A.
(June, 1992)

It was a steamy Friday morning in August, 1965, when, as a state parole officer, I pulled my state-issued Studebaker Lark up to the four-story apartment building on 103rd Street in Los Angeles to deliver an "early discharge" to a parolee. I was aware that there had been a "disturbance" the previous night, about a mile away, when California Highway Patrol officers had "scuffled" with persons being arrested for traffic violations; but I did not connect that incident with the large crowds gathering on the street corners.

I walked into the Watts District Police Substation, next door to the apartment building, and asked the desk officer what was going on. In response, he asked if I was armed. I was not. He suggested that I "get the hell out" of there, and I did. Thirty minutes later, the substation was under siege, and the Watts riots were under way.

Understandable, then, was the sense of *Deja vu* when rioting erupted a few weeks ago after the verdict in the Rodney King beating trial was announced. These were the same streets I drove in 1965, the same scenes of looting and fires and troops. But there were differences: this time television was there, showing live what we could see only on the horizon from our Lynwood home, about a mile from Watts. And this time, as hard as it was to believe, the violence and destruction was even worse.

The latter difference was graphically brought home with the scenes, videotaped "live" from a helicopter, of a man being pulled from his truck and beaten. That could have been me, I knew, if there had been the same propensity for violence in 1965. After seeing that scene I found myself avoiding news reports on the riots.

But one cannot avoid, cannot forget, cannot repress. The memories are too vivid, the danger too real. We must pay attention, before it is too late. And we must resist the temptation to over-simplify, to offer "solutions" based on misperceptions of the problems. Despite the urge to "rush to action," solutions based on misunderstanding will at best do nothing to help, and may well make things worse.

With these thoughts in mind, I offer the following "observations," not so much to provide solutions as to suggest perspectives that may be helpful in our attempts to understand:

In trying to understand the trial jury's decision, we must realize that our judicial system is *not* about "justice," as we would ordinarily think of the term. Trials do not "find" truth, they "determine" it. Trials are structured processes in which rules (derived through the centuries from English common law) determine and limit how evidence is reviewed, how arguments are advanced, and how decisions are made. The results of the process are "accepted" as truth (i.e., as justice) unless some procedural rules are determined to have been violated. Whatever the Simi Valley jury decided, then, *was* "justice," even if it was *not* "just."

I believe that the state of relations between blacks and whites in this country are, in fact, much worse today than they were during the 1960s. Although there may be many more opportunities for minorities today, the "gulf" between the affluent, mostly white, communities and the poor, largely minority, communities is greater than ever. Prejudice, stereotyping, and segregation are just as pervasive as thirty years ago. And there is added to the highly combustible mix the results of thirty years of failure to keep promises, of denial of problems, even of policies that have directly served to make things worse.

I do not believe that non-minorities, even psychologists "trained" to listen and understand, can *possibly* understand the pervasiveness and intensity of the anger that erupted in south-central Los Angeles. It is much too simple to "shrug off" the burning and looting as "thugs and hoodlums." Over and over the media reported on ordinary persons caught up and acting out of rage they did not understand.

We have concocted a terrifying, explosive mixture out of prejudice, ignorance and disdain. We may have precious little time to prevent eruptions that would make the sixties look peaceful. But we must be careful we do not add even more fuel to the mix under the guise of misguided solutions.

On The Road to Waco
(April, 1993)

I moved to Waco, Texas, when I was 19, leaving the Missouri School of Mines in Rolla after a disastrous fifth semester, driving a 1951 Nash Rambler that looked like an upside-down bathtub but leaked when it rained. Everything I owned was in the Nash. I had no money, no job, no friends in Waco, and only the barest of plans. It was, looking back on it, either the closest I ever came to a "great adventure" or to foolishly running away.

My goal was Baylor University, the "world's largest Baptist university." I had only recently resolved my "adolescent angst" – my search for purpose – by joining a Baptist Church and deciding to "become a preacher." Baylor, of course, was where they prepared Baptist preachers. (In fact, the joke at Baylor was that you could always tell which students were the "preacher boys" – Baptists, at least at that time, didn't know about women preachers – because they were the ones bumping into trees when they were walking while reading their Bibles at the same time.)

My friends today would not be surprised to learn that I was not like the other religion students – I was never "sure enough" to be a good Baptist, I asked too many questions, and I avoided trees. But I did graduate with a BA in religion and a minor in New Testament Greek. (One never knows what one will need along the way!)

I've thought a lot about Waco recently while watching the stand-off at the Branch Davidian headquarters outside that city. After a murderous fire-fight when federal agents attempted to storm the headquarters building, more than 100 cult members, including several children, were surrounded for several weeks before being killed in a cataclysmic fire that erupted during a final federal attack.

The cult leader, who went by the name of David Koresh, was by all accounts charismatic, dominating, and irrational. He was accused of stockpiling an arsenal of illegal weapons, of having sex with and impregnating the underage daughters of cult members, and of believing that he was Jesus Christ.

The Waco situation raises many questions. Personally, I do not question the original "surprise-storm" strategy of the ATF agents. I assume, without additional information, that they had concluded that this was the best and safest strategy. In fact, I find it easier to question persons (such as one man heard on the radio) that condemned the government for "violating the 2nd amendment rights" of "peaceful" Branch Davidians, who just happened to have enough armaments to win the Gulf War without General Swartzkopf.

But how are we to understand David Koresh? Or, perhaps more to the point, how are we to understand his followers? Are we to really believe that several dozen reasonably sane persons actually believe that a man who collects guns, has sex with all the women and sings bad rock music is a god? Or are they *all* insane?

I was talking with a good friend and thoughtful observer, Robert Hoyer, about this a few days ago. Hoyer, a retired Lutheran minister, suggested that this situation demonstrates again the danger in believing in any absolute source of truth (such as another individual or, for that matter, the Bible). But why do any of us need absolute sources of truth? Our conversation led us to speculate that *truth,* or what is presented and perceived as truth, allays *anxiety*, which may explain why, in times of high societal anxiety, people will follow absolutely certain, albeit insane, charismatic leaders.

Hoyer, a theologian even though he denies it, went on to suggest that these ideas emphasized the value of *doubt.* The paradox may be that in accepting one's doubts one can have "faith" without the need for certainty. As a psychologist I recognize the same concept in one's capacity to *tolerate ambiguity.* That is, as my tolerance for ambiguity increases I need less certainty in my life to manage my anxiety.

So what about Waco? Waco was a watershed period in my life, when I began to become aware of who and what I was. It appears that Waco is a watershed in other lives as well. One can only hope that we will learn whatever lessons such events teach.

Without, of course, bumping into any of Baylor's trees.

Floods, Phillips 66, and the Theodicy Question
(September, 1993)

One of the "corporate victims" of this summer's flooding was Phillips 66, whose propane storage facility near the River Des Peres flooded, forcing the evacuation of several hundred non-flooded residents. Subsequent news reports documented the anger of many of these residents who felt Phillips was not adequately compensating them for their losses.

The residents' plight brought back painful memories: I was ten years old when a creek near our farm exploded into flames after a Phillips' natural gas pipeline, which ran under the creek, developed a leak. My father, who had gone down to the creek to help a man he knew pull his stalled care out of the water (there was no bridge), ended up in the burning water. He had attempted to rescue the other man, who had started the inferno either by trying to start his car or, perhaps, by lighting a cigarette. My father spent three weeks in the hospital while the other man, more severely burned, was there six. Both men were scarred for life as, psychologically, was I.

At issue in the River Des Peres controversy was the question of *responsibility*. The critical residents argued that Phillips was negligent in placing propane storage tanks by a river (even a drainage ditch masquerading as a river). The problem with this argument, it seems to me, is that it attempts to make *relative* issues *absolute*. I assume that Phillips placed the storage facility there because it was less residential and, therefore, judged to be less risky. After all, the storage facility had to be located *somewhere*.

But there is a larger issue of responsibility here. Who, after all, is accountable for the losses from the flood itself? Must the government (read that you and I, the taxpayers) rescue persons who chose to live in flood plains and thus were forced to evacuate, find temporary housing, clean up, and rebuild or relocate? A common theme on street corners, radio talk shows and in letters to editors has been how "those people" should assume the risk: they either should not live there, or should have insurance.

We are, I fear, a people condemned by three irrational convictions: we believe in simple solutions, we are quick to pass judgment, and we always assume someone must be to blame. Never mind the realities: that people live near rivers because they cannot afford safer housing; that, having too little money they cannot afford very expensive flood insurance; that moving out far enough to affordable housing would reduce already minimal opportunities to find work. People too poor to function effectively in our society, we know, must have done something to deserve it.

The short answer to the question of responsibility is that *certainly* persons living near rivers incur risks; and *certainly* we (as government) share in the responsibility to provide relief. We – you and I – are part of the complex society that has created poverty and that makes it so impossible for most persons in poverty to escape. For what it's worth, of course, you and I also incur risks living where we choose, with health hazards, from pollution, congestion and contagion; violence, encouraged at least in part by our consumption of violent media; and ever-present dangers, from cars on our streets, airplanes in our skies, or even earthquakes from the seismic fault we choose to live upon.

So, who *is* to blame? The ultimate question has to do with ultimate responsibility. The teen-aged girl who could not get to her session with me because the flooded river wiped out Highway 40 asked it best: "Why would God do this?" Unknowingly, this young woman was posing the *theodicy question*: why would a supposedly all-powerful God allow bad things to happen to people, especially people who believe?

Like all ultimate questions, of course, the theodicy question has no ultimate answer. Some, including many psychologists, would say the answer is that God is not all-powerful, or, perhaps, there is no God: evil is random. But all of us, one way or the other, need some sort of meaning and purpose in our lives. That is, after all, what belief in God provides.

Others have suggested that God allows evil to punish us for our sin: our failings, or perhaps our unbelief. But we know, of course, that evil is not proportionate to the misdeeds of the victims. Still others, more obliquely, suggest that God allows evil so we can appreciate grace, God's love, the healing potential of the creation. This is, in fact, the primary answer offered in contemporary Christian theology.

You may know that the theodicy question is the issue posed by the Bible's Book of Job. Coincidentally, as the flood waters were rising, I was just finishing reading *The First Dissident: The Book of Job in Today's Politics* by William Safire. It is recommended reading for anyone interested in the theodicy question.

Phillips 66 settled with my father and his fellow victim in 1948 for $6,000 and $24,000 respectively. Even given 45 years' inflation, those amounts were paltry compared to multi-million dollar settlements imposed by courts today. Perhaps the question for our time is not *who* is responsible?" but "what is the *price* of responsibility?"

A Depressing Tale of Terror
(April, 1997)

All right, I'll admit that Stephen King can write a pretty scary book, especially if you buy his off-the-wall premises; but his stuff is, after all, fiction. If you *really* enjoy horror pick up *A Civil Action* by Jonathan Harr (Vintage Books, 1995).

I haven't read anything this frightening (and depressing) since *And The Band Played On* (St. Martin's Press, 1987), Randy Shilts' terrifying description of how the AIDS epidemic spread while everyone – the government, the media, the scientific community, and even the Gay community – delayed, denied and demagogued. *A Civil Action* won the 1995 National Book Critics Circle Award for nonfiction. It's the fact that it is nonfiction, ultimately, that makes it so frightening.

Each year when Marilyn and I make our pilgrimage to Boston we rent a car at Logan Airport, survive the drive through the Sullivan Tunnel and hop on I-93 heading north toward Winchester, the close-in suburb where Marilyn grew up. Hanging a left at Route 128 we exit at Washington Street and drive south, through Woburn, toward Winchester. This route takes us along the Aberjona River and past the industrial plants of W. R. Grace and the Riley Tannery, a division of Beatrice Foods. Between Washington Street and the Tannery, along the River, lies a 15 acre plot adjacent to City property on which were two water wells that once serviced eastern Woburn.

Once, as we drove down Washington, Marilyn mentioned that her family had owned property "over there" – pointing in the direction of the Tannery. She remembered going there with her father once for firewood. "A funny thing happened, though," she said; "After my father's death my mother realized she had not gotten a tax bill for the property for some years." Apparently the City of Woburn had appropriated the property. My mother-in-law considered legal action, but decided against it when she heard rumors of industrial pollution in that area.

Sounds like a good move: the area became the focus of the largest environmental pollution civil suit in U.S. history.

In the mid-1960s Woburn, which obtained its water from local wells, responded to a chronic summer shortage by drilling two wells east of the Aberjona River. Almost immediately local residents began complaining about the water, which developed a strong "chemical" taste and smell, and which was often discolored. City engineers repeatedly checked the water and pronounced it "potable," which, apparently, means "safe to drink" in municipal water-talk.

In the early 1970s eastern Woburn began to experience a surprisingly large number of cases of childhood leukemia. In addition, residents complained frequently of rashes and other ailments. Gradually, the water supply began to attract suspicion, and in particular, the water from the two local wells.

Eventually accusing fingers were pointed at W. R. Grace, which used TCE, (trichloroethelyne) and other chemicals known to be carcinogenic in laboratory animals in its paint shop; and the Riley Tannery, which used similar chemicals in treating animal hides. Both plants were accused of dumping polluted wastes into the ground, ditches or pits on or near their properties.

In the early 1980s a strange character became involved in the case. Jan Schlichtmann, a flamboyant young personal injury lawyer with a reputation for winning big cases, filed suit on behalf of nine Woburn families against Grace and Beatrice Foods. Schlichtmann's style was aggressive, thorough, and expensive. Less than half-way through the trial he had spent almost three million dollars – money neither he nor his firm had – on the investigation, discovery, and trial.

By the summer of 1986 Schlichtmann and his associates were out of money and credit, with everything they possessed mortgaged or repossessed; family members were fighting one another; and Schlichtmann was obsessed to the point of madness. Meanwhile Grace and Beatrice, two of the country's largest corporations, showed no signs of giving up their patterns of denial, obstruction and delay.

A Civil Action is a depressing indictment of a legal system we like to call "the best in the world," but which best serves the interests of those who can pay to make it work for themselves. It is also an indictment of a corporate America which too often allows dollars to determine its morality. In the end, although gripping, it is a chilling and depressing tale; but it is recommended reading for anyone considering using the legal system to confront corporate or bureaucratic abuse.

Read it on a rainy day, when you're likely to be depressed anyway.

Uncle Guido and the Corporate Loan Sharks
(November, 1997)

A former client was given to laughingly fantasizing that she could solve her problems by looking up her "Uncle Guido," presumably a knuckle-buster for a local loan shark. "Uncle Guido" was her humorous way of acknowledging that there were some problems that she could not solve herself, that she must simply live through.

Most of us do not have access to an "Uncle Guido," and my hope is that none of us would resort to such methods if we did. Furthermore, one could hope that there is little market for such services in today's America: after all, there are no longer loan sharks, are there?

Unfortunately, there are. And, like the mobs that might have given Uncle Guido his vocation, today's loan sharks seem to have gone legitimate: that is, they now dress in three-piece suits and work in corporate offices. Even more distressing, you and I – almost every one of us – are their customers.

Their corporate names are generic: you know them as any one of a number of credit cards, or a growing proliferation of other lenders. Their "scam," if you will, is pulling in unwitting victims, loading them with debt, and then casting them aside. Credit card companies repeatedly send applications for new cards to college students with no income, or to individuals with maxed-out cards; and a recent report documents lending agencies' practices of sending unsolicited "checks," which, if signed and cashed, become loans at absurd interest rates.

It is time we call spades spades.

Seldom does a month go by when I do not get at least one document from Bankruptcy Court reflecting the filing or processing of bankruptcy proceedings by one of my current or past clients. And, although I have certainly worked with clients with spending or gambling problems, these have not been the clients taking bankruptcy. Bankruptcy has become many clients' only option because of accumulated debt and reduced earning capacity due to chronic illness or disability, not excess unwise spending.

A vivid example is Jeannine (not her real name), who was released from a hospital psychiatric unit to live alone in an apartment building in South County despite having no family in the area; no income or job; no means of transportation, and in an area with very limited public transportation; and despite having a sizable debt (the unpaid portion of her hospital bill).

The fact that the hospital social service department arranged such a release is disappointing, but not surprising. Social workers have to arrange some kind of release; and Jeannine did have distant family elsewhere in South County – although they were not reachable by public transportation, and not really very willing to help.

The only way Jeannine could pay her rent and eat, to say nothing of the monthly hospital payments, was to use her one credit card. All too soon she had run the balance to its limit, and found that her minimum monthly payment was only covering the interest. Worse yet, she still had bills and no income.

Ah, but, not to worry: her friendly neighborhood credit card companies (located in Delaware, California, or some other far-away place) were more than willing to provide higher credit limits or new cards.

Almost overnight, it seemed, her debt became staggering, and she could not pay the collected minimum payments – which did not even cover the collected interest accumulation – each month without resorting yet again to even newer credit cards willingly supplied by the same card companies. And, yes, these were the same companies that, at the same time, were referring her to collection agencies to collect her arrears debt with emotionally devastating harassment.

If this is not loan sharking, it's close enough for me. By whatever name it is unconscionable. Equally unconscionable, I'm afraid, is the failure by "good" people like you and me, people who profess to care about others, who are educated enough to differentiate between economic necessity and corporate loan-sharking, but who still do nothing to call attention to the problem. Or, for that matter, who fail to call attention to the prejudicial stereotyping of individuals forced to resort to bankruptcy.

It has been said that the true measure of a society lies in the way it handles its dispossessed, its criminals and its poor. If this is true, we are a sorry lot indeed.

We'd be better off with Uncle Guido.

Odd Ends

Odd Ends

I have always had a "sense of the absurd," a capacity to recognize the bizarre in otherwise ordinary life experiences. It is, I suspect, what has helped me survive, the gift of a God that recognizes that life itself is absurd.

I learned early on to hold this gift private. Sharing absurdity certainly demands more safety than I ever knew as a child. In recent years, however, I have learned to work with it, contain it, smooth its harsh surfaces and sharp edges, and even let it occasionally be seen.

At the same time, I have always carried a need to make sense of things, to understand the "reasons why." We humans seem to have this need built-in, "hard wired." In all probability this developed early in our evolution as a species, a naturally-selected capacity for survival by recognizing threatening patterns from previous experience.

As a result, we do not handle "randomness" well. Regardless of the event: disease, pestilence, or act of nature, we will try to organize and explain it. Sometimes we are successful: diabetes, it turns out, runs in families; severe storms are impacted by water temperature in the South Pacific. Other times we impose meaning where there is none: if all else fails there is always "conspiracy" or, perhaps, "God's will."

Finding meaning in randomness is, I suppose, a good example of "taking things too seriously," *working too hard* at life. In point of fact much of life *is* random, or at least disconnected and inexplicable. And it is certainly the case that much of it is just absurd.

Some things just defy explanation. In a word, the world *is* full of "*odd ends.*"

The Media Biz
(May, 1990)

The life of a media celebrity can be very hard.

Every time there is a serious air crash my telephone rings. Although once in a while the caller is a former "fearful flyer" client seeking reassurance, more often it is a producer or reporter from a local radio or television station wanting to know if this crash "will affect fearful flyers."

It seems a bit morbid to use a tragedy to get publicity, and it certainly reflects a limited view of what I do in my practice; but publicity is publicity and I keep hoping they will let me say more about what I really do. So, after the recent United Airlines disaster I agreed to appear on the "Morning Show" on Channel 5.

The good news was that I would be interviewed by anchor Jennifer Blome. The bad news was that the interview was to be in the 6:10 AM interview segment.

And so I began to do the essentials: clear my calendar (not difficult at 6:00 AM); set the alarm (and check it twice; you really *can* set a clock radio for 4:00 AM!); decide what to wear; think about the important things I wanted to say during the interview. . . . In spite of all this activity I *did* drift off to sleep – only to be awakened at some indeterminate hour when Marilyn sat upright in bed wondering "why is the clock dark?"

The clock was dark because it was an electric clock radio, and there wasn't any electricity. Again, good news and bad news: it was only 3:25 AM; but this was going to be a shower and shave from memory. Fortunately, I could retrieve the clothing I had picked out the previous evening, providing I did not set the closet on fire with my candle. Is this how Bryant Gumbel does it?

It *was* fascinating to watch the Channel 5 newsroom crew at work. Being a slow news day, I was only knocked aside two times by the producer racing "Broadcast News" style through the green room (which, for whatever it is worth, is not green).

Jennifer Blome is even more attractive in person than on television. The segment lasted two minutes or less, but I was verbally coherent, and the producer and anchors seemed pleased. Even a psychiatrist friend, obviously an early riser, called later to applaud.

But will it do any good? Is it worthwhile to drive 50 miles before dawn for less than two minutes? Will anyone learn that their panic about flying can be helped? Will I get any calls in response?

My experience has been that there will be few, if any, calls in direct response to the program, although months later someone may tell me that they "saw me on TV." And there may be some increased public awareness that there are programs for fearful flyers and, more generically, that psychologists help people.

I do wonder, though, if brief "sound bites" on serious problems may not serve only to trivialize, contributing to the perception that complex problems can be assessed and corrected in two minutes. And I wonder what misperceptions are fostered by the media's focus only on the dramatic (air disasters) or the titillating (any subject with "sex" in the title).

The fantasy, of course, is that when the interview segment is over the beautiful anchor-person will whisper "call me later today; I'd like to set up an appointment." It didn't happen, but it is still a nice fantasy.

Buzz Me, Little Hal!
(April, 1995)

My laptop computer, HAL Jr., reconfigured itself one day last week. In a moment of apparent Intel psychosis, perhaps designed to permit quiet internal reflection, it disabled its communication ports and its 3.5 inch floppy disk drive, deciding to interact only through a 5.25 inch drive, which it does not have.

I first became aware of the problem when I discovered that HAL Jr. would not allow its mouse to appear out of its cybernetic mouse hole. Unfortunately, after struggling through Windows by keyboard and typing for 45 minutes I realized that HAL was rejecting *all* communication with the outside world. I thought I heard laughter, but one can never be sure with computers.

I am a product of a by-gone era. As a child, radio (AM, yet!) was hi-tech. My father, a prejudiced man with a sense of humor, loved to listen to Amos & Andy, a program in which two white men played black characters with, by today's standards, totally unacceptable stereotypes. One of the characters, Andy, had a wonderful bass voice which my father loved to imitate. Andy ran a business with, apparently, no business. He had a secretary, Miss Blue, and a somewhat limited telephone system. Periodically, to talk with his secretary, or to appear busier that he really was, Andy would call out, "Oh, Miss Blue! Buzz me!"

I could not help but think of Andy and Miss Blue last week when I engaged yet another technological advance: I became "wired." Yes, ashamed as I am to admit it, I am now "connected." I have joined the "now" generation. I have acquired a pager, which I call "Hal III," or "Little Hal".

I have long resisted pagers and other forms of mobile communication. Years ago, in a galaxy far away, known as Los Angeles, I was a parole agent. Since we spent much of our time "in the field," driving around looking for parolees who were driving around looking for ways to avoid us, the idea of two-way car radios was raised. I objected. "Why would I want to talk to anyone when I'm in the car?" I asked. "That's the only time I'm free!"

My objection to pagers has been equally emphatic, although more psychological. A pager, I argued, would change the nature of my practice, inevitably increasing the number of emergencies as clients became aware that I was more accessible. With more immediate information, especially delivered with an urgent-sounding *beep!* I would begin treating in-coming information as more critical, thereby conspiring to create emergencies. I would, in effect, be enabling "emergaholic" clients (a wonderful word I, myself, just coined).

In truth, I suspect my arguments were based on reasonable observations but poor conclusions. Certainly, some colleagues I have observed with pagers have had more emergencies; but they may well have had more emergencies even if they had not had pagers, either because of the nature of their caseloads (and sources of referrals) or their personalities and therapy styles. The causative agent, in other words, was more likely to be client or therapist characteristics than pagers.

Furthermore, the truth of the matter is that *my* caseload has become more crisis-prone even *without* a pager as I have acquired more, and more disturbed, clients. There have been too many instances of my returning home late in the evening after the Symphony or some other cultural event, like a party to a message of an emergency call several hours earlier. I have actually come to view the absence of a blinking light on my answering machine upon arriving at home as a positive sign, the absence of an emergency, rather than a negative sign, that my kids and grandkids don't love me.

So I have a pager. Being constitutionally unobtrusive I have it set on "vibrate," which the salesperson, a flirtatious young woman with beautiful brown eyes, termed "silent," and which has the primary effect, when it signals, of causing me to think that something has gone neurological wrong with part of my anatomy.

Interestingly, the primary initial effect I have observed thus far is a *reduction* in messages. I am assuming that this result is a statistical artifact (that is, an old statistic dug up, presumably, by archaeologists), but, of course, one can never be sure with pagers.

Meanwhile, if you need me, call. Little Hal will buzz me right away!

The Weekend from Hell
(March, 1996)

To start with, it was the "weekend from hell." First, there was the cold – not the temperature, the virus. I came down with it Wednesday evening, and by Thursday was well beyond miserable. Marilyn succumbed Thursday evening, pointedly blaming me despite what we both knew about required incubation periods. By the weekend we were single-handedly – actually, doublehandedly – responsible for a several point jump in the value of Kleenex stock.

Then there was the cold -- not the virus, the temperature: the coldest in recent recorded history. It was a good weekend to stay in, which was pretty much all we could do anyway. I did take the already-prepared salad to the Friday night video pot-luck, but I fell asleep in the middle of "The Madness of King George" and never did quite figure out who or what was going on. And there *was* the scheduled "Responsible Psychotherapy" Task Force meeting scheduled for Sunday in Columbia, but things certainly could have been worse.

And they got worse Friday night when I awoke for my scheduled 2:00 AM bathroom run and realized the power was off in our all-electric home. Deluding myself into thinking this was a temporary aberration I fell back asleep, only to reawaken at 4:00 AM with the realization that my dream of freezing to death was not a dream.

Fortunately we had flashlights (easily found), candles (finally located), oil lamps (not useful at all until I awoke Marilyn because the oil was in the only cabinet I *didn't* look in); and wood for the fireplace (although it was a cold trip out to the patio to access it). So I can report that we did not freeze to death, which is comforting, although the whole weekend was pretty well messed up.

I can also report that Union Electric was satisfactorily responsive, although I did find my 4:00 AM conversation with UE's computer disconcerting. About 6:30 AM I heard noises outside and, putting on every bit of clothing I could locate, emerged to find Chewbacca, or at least a repairman wearing a ski hat that looked like Harrison Ford's Wookie from "Star Wars," completing work on the failed transformer in front of the house. By 7:00 AM the power was on, but the damage (at least the psychological damage) was already done.

Which was why I probably *should not* have tried to install the new modem in my computer on Saturday. I rationalized that I needed the modem because the CompuServe program I wanted to down-load to become an Internet surfer would have taken five hours with the old modem. Actually, by the time I put in the new modem CompuServe had already sent an upgrade that made the downloading unnecessary, which I at first misread as a positive sign.

It turned out that the new CompuServe program took up all the space on my obviously hopelessly inadequate hard drive, so there was insufficient space (or was it memory?) to get on CompuServe, so the new modem was pretty much useless. The solution, obviously, would be a newer, larger hard drive and more memory or, of course, just buying postage.

We recently ran into a similar problem at the office, where we installed a billing system to become more efficient and impress our less sophisticated therapist friends. Within weeks we became dependent on the new system, so when our "hardware support" person, the guy who sold us the system, told us we faced a "crash" if we did not upgrade our hard drive (have you noticed how *terrifying* computer terminology is?) we rushed in with our checkbook.

The computer store actually installed an even larger drive than recommended (not out of generosity but because that's all they had available), but then the billing system, which had started the whole problem, wouldn't run on the new drive. Turns out the billing system likes to hang out in the same part of the computer that was being used to run the new, improved, and larger, hard drive, and it apparently got its cybernetic nose out of joint. This, of course, is not technical talk; I am simplifying the problem for the non-computer-literate.

We finally fixed the problem using the latest technology. We hypnotized the damn hard drive and convinced it that it was not as big as it really was, so we didn't need the trespassing software and the billing system could return to its old neighborhood. No technology is going to get the better of us!

Is there a point to this? Yes there is. Unfortunately, it's buried in the part of the computer we repressed hypnotically.

As for me, I'm going back to carbon paper.

Technology & the Afterlife
(November, 1996)

I was recently introduced, through a discussion group, to Ernest Becker's Pulitzer Prize-winning monograph *The Denial of Death*. Becker's hypothesis, that the fundamental source of human anxiety lies in the fact that we are conscious animals, and thus capable of awareness that there will come a time when we *will not be,* resonated powerfully. My initial impression has been that this book is, in fact, one of the most important of its time, well deserving of the Pulitzer.

One might wonder how I could have missed such an important book when it was first published, but in 1973 I was a first-year faculty member teaching four new criminal justice courses, working on my dissertation, and trying to cope with kids, a new city, and life in general (as well as being just out of graduate school and in a decidedly "anti-psychological-reading" frame of mind), so I suppose it's not surprising that I might have avoided such an anxiety-provoking book – which was, now that I think about it, Becker's thesis in the first place.

Reflecting on Becker's ideas led me to recall earlier, post-adolescent, attempts to rationalize the dilemma of "thinking about not being," at a time when I sought answers within a narrow, or at least more narrow than I would pursue today, theological framework. "The reason I believe in life after death," I remember telling some unremembered person, "is because I cannot conceive of a time when I cease to exist!" It is, Becker suggests, the ultimate curse of humanity -- to be only an animal, and finite, *and know it.*

A colleague and I were enjoying one of those wide-ranging conversations over lunch the other day (an all-too-rare experience for two private-practice types!) when Becker's book came up. We had each been talking about the things we wanted to do but couldn't because we were too busy (yes, we had been bemoaning managed care!), like "learn a foreign language," or "read for fun" or, in my case, "write the great American novel." Somewhat facetiously I suggested that I was looking forward to the time, after death, when there would finally be time for such activities.

It's a bizarre thought, I suppose, and perhaps a little morbid, but, like all bizarre ideas can lead to intriguing places if one "runs with it." And run we did: soon exploring the implications of equipping the casket with a lap-top, with a fax/modem, of course, and a telephone jack so we could connect to the Internet. The possibilities are endless.

You may recall that Harry Houdini promised to "send messages back" from the great beyond; but as far as I know, no transmissions were ever received. Perhaps the problem wasn't Houdini's idea, but that he was ahead of the technology: he had no fax/modem, lap-top, or software. Any day now I expect some enterprising software company to announce *Celestial,* with a built-in translator from EOS ("Eternal Operating System") to Windows or Mac.

Writing the novels so many of us think we have hidden inside would be a piece of cake -- we'd have plenty of time to think things through (as well as for rewrites), and wouldn't have to worry about what anybody else thought about what we'd said. And you thought Salmon Rushdie was well-hidden after *Satanic Verses!*

An Internet browser would be essential, of course. Not only for e-mail (we'd finally be able to tell all those pompous friends and infuriating family members exactly what we thought!), but we'd want to keep up on world and national events. You can find anything on the Internet if you know how to search and have enough time, so we'd finally be able to actually learn about the issues and candidates *before* an election. And, when "voting by Internet" finally comes, we'd even be able to exercise our franchise!

Come to think of it, they've been doing something similar in Chicago for years.

Yes, I know Ernest Becker would say I'm simply proving his point, that death – not existing – is so fearful a prospect that we will go to any extreme to deny its reality; but, really, now, would you have stayed with a whole page of anxiety-provoking reality about *not-being?* Who ever said all defense mechanisms were bad, anyway?

Let's see. . . I'll need a night-light, and plenty of RAM, and a *big* box of floppy disks . . . .

Undaunted Courage
(January, 1998)

You have to understand, in the beginning, that my wife Marilyn and I differ when it comes to water. Marilyn grew up loving the water, living in a suburb of Boston and summering on Cape Anne. I, on the other hand, grew up hydrophobic in the Midwest. Marilyn's idea of a perfect vacation would be a windjammer cruise. I am the student who, after the swimming instructor fished me out of the pool, was responsible for the Missouri School of Mines' dropping their requirement that all students pass a swimming test.

Opposites attract, I suppose.

So you can appreciate that our plan to take a river cruise up the Columbia-Snake Rivers in honor of Marilyn's surviving 25 years of marriage with me would be an adventure, in differing ways, for each of us. Marilyn looked forward to the week-long trip on a small cruise ship with growing anticipation.

In my own way, I was also excited: I began reading *Undaunted Courage: Meriwether Lewis, Thomas Jefferson, and the Opening of the American West,* Stephen Ambrose' marvelous account of the 1804-06 Lewis and Clark expedition. I also updated my will and packed my cute little floppy "vacation hat" which Marilyn had bought me for *our* annual trips to Cape Anne.

I am here, a cruise survivor, to tell you that the trip was wonderful, even with the Northwest Territory's ubiquitous rain. The "Spirit of Columbia" is a small ship operated by Alaska Sightseeing/Cruise West, which operates similar cruises to Alaska, through the Inland Waters, and to other sites. The ship was quite comfortable, with surprisingly spacious cabins ("staterooms," in the lexicon of the cruise), excellent food, and a young, enthusiastic and entertaining crew.

The cruise was organized around the Lewis and Clark Expedition, which was designed, in large part, to find a "water route" across the American West from the confluence of the Missouri River at the Mississippi to the mouth of the Columbia River at the Pacific. When planning was begun President Thomas Jefferson was trying to build a *prima-facia* basis for American claims in the trans-Mississippi region, which he recognized was the inevitable direction of American migration. By the time Lewis and Clark departed from St. Louis, however, Jefferson had purchased the Louisiana Territory from Napoleon; but there were still vast areas of uncertain ownership.

As a Virginia landowner, in an era when land was farmed to exhaustion and then abandoned, Jefferson recognized the value of new land open for the taking, if one ignored any claims the Native Americans might have to prior occupancy. He also recognized the potential of Meriwether Lewis, a Virginia neighbor, an experienced woodsman with military experience, and an avid learner, as a leader of the expedition. Lewis brought in his friend William Clark as co-leader; and together they recruited and carefully prepared a remarkably capable crew.

The problem, of course, was that the Missouri River headwaters and the Columbia headwaters (identified on our maps as the Snake River because they were located from the east) do not meet. In fact, they are separated by miles of rugged, and in winter impassable, mountains – a geographic reality unknown to Jefferson and Lewis but well known to local Native Americans. One of the most interesting aspects of the expedition was how unwilling Lewis and Clark were to trust the expertise of the native residents; and how remarkably adept they were at antagonizing them by offering them cheap gifts, when what they wanted were guns and whisky!

Lewis and Clark ended up sailing down the Snake and Columbia Rivers, so our trip up and down the same rivers had special meaning. Of course, we traversed the Bitterroot Mountains at 35,000 feet, a much easier trip than theirs. But we were still able to cover similar ground, visit the same sites, and even stand in the reconstructed Fort Clatsop where they wintered, near the mouth of the Columbia, in 1806. These experiences, together with Ambrose' wonderful account, brought meaning to his phrase *Undaunted Courage,* as well as a deeper appreciation of our national heritage.

On Tuesday morning, as I was hurrying from our cabin to catch the jet boats that would take us through Hell's Canyon, a gust of wind carried my cute little vacation hat into the river. The last I saw of it was a salmon wearing it upstream to spawn.

Like Meriwether Lewis, I also gave something of myself to the River. Undaunted courage, indeed!

Ode to a Black Cat
(August, 2000)

He came into the family one Sunday afternoon, carried into the house by 16-year-old Stephanie: coal black, about six weeks old, big intelligent-looking eyes.

"He jumped into the car when we stopped at the drug store," Stephanie lied, straight-faced. "Right!" I replied. "How far did you have to chase him across the parking lot to get him to jump into the car?"

I'm not sure anyone actually discussed his staying; it was just assumed. The only dissenter was Melly, our "Lassie" collie. Melly spent the first evening at the bottom of a flight of stairs, barking furiously, while the sleek black kitten crouched half-way up, hissing. But when we arrived home the next afternoon the kitten was curled between Melly's front legs, being groomed, proving again that mothering instincts outweigh genus differences.

Steph named him "Ozzie." In his prime, Oz was a beautiful animal: pure black, with a large, leopard-like head, and big, beautiful eyes. Being male, he liked to roam, usually returning within a day or two. But a year or so after adopting us he went out one May morning and did not return until October.

We assumed, of course, that he was gone -- lost, hit by a car, or taken in by another family. A few nights before Halloween Marilyn had a dream: Ozzie was at the door, trailing six or seven black kittens, asking to come in. The next morning he was there, at the back door.

Two days later a kitten, totally black except for a white spot on her neck, was crying at the same door. With us still, her name is "Izzy." (Creativity in names was never Stephanie's strong point: she once named a kitten, obtained from the Richmond, Virginia animal shelter on her sixth birthday, "Birthday.")

After his summer away Ozzie was never the same. For one thing, he had lost his "meow" somewhere, presumably from an infection. In addition, he was easily "spooked:" strange shapes or sounds would send him scurrying.

But he was always affectionate. A sitting lap was irresistible; and he loved nothing more than curling at your head, if you were lying down, kneading and licking your hair. (Unless the ceiling fan was on: Oz was terrified of blades turning above his head.)

Like most cats, Ozzie loved to get "above the fray," usually greeting us from the top of a living-room chair, or the kitchen counter if we were coming in from the garage. And he made every attempt to cook an ordeal, investigating everything. Especially fish: Oz would crawl into the oven with a tuna-fish casserole.

In short, Ozzie was a *presence* around the house: sometimes manic, sometimes loving, but always *imposing*. Much like Samantha Morton in Woody Allen's "Sweet and Lowdown," Ozzie demonstrated that one does not need a voice to make an impact.

Ozzie did not age well, perhaps because of his youthful exploits. At about twelve he developed kidney problems, and in one episode lost all the hair on his tail (creating an interesting effect: a black cat with a rat's tail). Gradually, he became thinner, slower, shakier, although still affectionate, and still excitable.

Finally, inevitably, the day came when it was apparent the end was near – curled up in an out-of-the-way spot, skin and bones, he had stopped eating and seemed only to be waiting.

After much anguish (mostly on my part; my wife, a hospice worker, seems more accepting of death), I called the vet. I say "I" – even though Marilyn was there at every step – because *I* needed to make the call, needed to take him, needed to be with him at the end. In part, I suppose, this was because I have always identified Ozzie with Stephanie, who brought him into the family, giving him special meaning.

But mostly, I think, I needed to be there because I have always run away from death, have always been terrified, and needed – *knew* that I needed – to embrace Ozzie's death so I could begin to embrace my own eventual end.

And so it was that Ozzie, that beautiful black cat with the huge, intelligent eyes, passed into the great "feline beyond" – gone, but never forgotten – tightly locked in my tearful embrace.

It's funny, I suppose, but often we don't realize what we learn from someone, or something, until they're gone. Looking back, I realize how much I've learned from an old black cat – a lot about living and, especially, a lot about dying.

Shalom, Oz.

A Last Look

ArJay at Sixty
(March, 1998)

When I was thirty years old, in the first of what some would say was to become a continuing series of mid-life crises, I uprooted my family to move half-way across the country for graduate school. In the process I gave up a career-track position with the California Department of Corrections to become a graduate assistant, and we moved our three children from a three-bedroom suburban home into a two-bedroom student apartment. Within a year the marriage had come apart at the seams.

I was reminded of this the other evening when I was asked whether I was having a "mid-life crisis." The question, from another student in the "Memoir Writing" class I am taking at Washington University, came as I explained the role I see the class playing in the "life-style changes" I am trying to make.

It was a reasonable question, I suppose, except that sixty hardly seems to qualify as mid-life; and any changes I am working on now are intentional, not crises-driven. I'm looking for ways to shift gears, work a little less, and do a little writing, not for a young wife and a new sports car. "Believe me," I said, "I've had many mid-life crises in my day. This isn't one of them!"

But I *am* one of the older students in the Memoir Writing class; the youngest is a college sophomore of about twenty. And a sixtieth birthday seems to demand reflection.

I have observed that birthdays ending in "zero," at least after one becomes 21, are especially significant. Until one approaches fifty they are events for looking forward, thinking about future goals and plans. At fifty I found myself looking both forward and backward, something of a "mid-course assessment." At sixty there seems to be more need for reflection, for coming to terms with the past. Any thoughts about the future have more to do with settling in to the world I have created than to conquering new ones.

So what can I say about sixty? One of the books Rockwell Gray assigned for his Memoir Writing class is *Coming into the End Zone* by Doris Grumbach (Norton, 1993). As Grumbach approached her seventieth year she began a journal. Her observations are at times uplifting and at times depressing, although always perceptive and full of wit, as she struggles to come to terms with the effects of age and infirmity. What would my journal – should I begin one – reflect?

A young client recently bemoaned approaching thirty. Her life is a mess. She cannot find intimacy with her husband, and is mired in a relationship that she is coming to recognize offers no hope. "I can only hope that my thirties will be better than my twenties," she said wistfully. I assured her that they could be; and that, for me, at least, my fifties were the best yet.

To be honest, though, fifty-nine has not been a picnic. Several months of painful sciatica and a wrenching upheaval within the small church we attend have made the past year trying at best. Overall, though, the last several years have made it possible for me to work on coming to terms with who I am and have been; and to grow as a person, a husband and father, and a psychologist.

And there are positive signs for the future.

In spite of managed care I have been able to work as much as I wish; and it looks as if I will be able to continue to gradually "cut back" while still maintaining a viable practice. Meanwhile, I am discovering new and exciting ways to write things – both personal and professional – I have always wanted to say.

I've also been feeling better physically. Over the past few weeks my sciatica has dramatically improved, and I can now do most of the things I could do a year ago. With care, I think, leisurely strolls and museums – even Laumeier Sculpture Park! – can be possible again.

And I may even be getting the hang of this "relationship" thing. Marilyn and I were invited to a New Year's Eve party this year, where the hostess proposed that we share our "wishes for the coming year." I am uncomfortable in those kinds of situations, and I mumbled something about plans for writing. Marilyn – usually not given to public expressions at all – was surprisingly positive about the year ahead, commenting in the process how much she enjoyed being married to me.

It was totally unexpected and, for a lonely kid never really sure he could be loved, without question the best sixtieth birthday present I could hope to get.

Viva la sixty!

Ron Scott is a retired psychologist living with his wife, Marilyn, in Kirkwood, Missouri. He has worked as a welfare worker, parole officer, work release center supervisor, university teacher, and private-practice pyschotherapist. Ron and Marilyn have a blended family, with five married children and eight grandchildren.